A
WOMAN'S
WALK IN
GRACE

CATHERINE MARTIN

A
WOMAN'S
WALK IN
GRACE

HARVEST HOUSE PUBLISHERS
EUGENE, OREGON

Cover by Koechel Peterson & Associates, Inc., Minneapolis, Minnesota

Cover photo © Stockxpert / Jupiter Images Unlimited

Catherine Martin: Published in association with the literary agency of WordServe Literary Group, Ltd., 10152 S. Knoll Circle, Highlands Ranch, CO 80130

A WOMAN'S WALK IN GRACE

Copyright © 2010 by Catherine Martin
Published by Harvest House Publishers
Eugene, Oregon 97402
www.harvesthousepublishers.com

Library of Congress Cataloging-in-Publication Data
  Martin, Catherine
  A woman's walk in grace / Catherine Martin.
    p. cm.
  ISBN 978-0-7369-2380-4 (pbk.)
  1. Grace (Theology) 2. Christian women—Religious life. I. Title.
  BT761.3.M29 2010
  248.8'43—dc22
                                                    2009027528

Printed in the United States of America

10 11 12 13 14 15 16 17 18 / VP-NI / 10 9 8 7 6 5 4 3 2 1

To my brother,
Robert Joseph Snyder—
You are a magnificent trophy of God's grace.

Rob, I admire you and love watching you pour out God's
grace on others around you. You are one of God's greatest gifts
of grace to me and the best brother any sister could have.

Thank you for loving me and encouraging me
to always believe God for the impossible.
I love you.

Acknowledgments

I'd like to thank the Lord for pouring out His grace on me, saving me, giving me His Word and His indwelling Spirit, and enabling me to grow in His incredible garden of grace. Because of His grace, I also want to say thank you to several other people.

To my amazing husband, David Martin, for constantly gracing me with God's love.

To my wonderful family—Mother, Dad, Robert, Tanya, Kayla, Christopher, Eloise, Andy, Keegan, and James—for consistently believing in my dreams and aspirations.

To the Quiet Time Ministries team—Kayla and Charlie Branscum, Cindy Clark, Paula Zillmer, Shirley Peters, Sandy Fallon, Myra Murphy, Julie Airis, Betty Mann, and Kelly Abeyratne—for sharing the joy of ministry with me as we serve the Lord together. Kayla, thank you for your humble attitude and steadfast faith. Cindy Clark, thank you for sharing my dreams.

To the Quiet Time Ministries board of directors and Quiet Time ministry partners, for your prayers and partnership in this ministry.

To Beverly Trupp, for sharing your home as I wrote this book and especially for your friendship. To Conni Hudson, for your love and encouragement. To Stefanie Kelly, for your incredible music. To Dottie McDowell, Vonette Bright, and Ney Bailey, for showing us all what grace looks like.

To Jim Smoke, for your wisdom and experience of many years as an author and pastor. To Greg Johnson of WordServe Literary, for your wisdom and help in all my books as we work together to share them with people around the world.

To the women of Southwest Community Church, for standing together with me for Jesus every day. To the SCC ministry team, for your daily fellowship and accountability. To Shelley Smith, for your tireless service for the Lord.

To the entire Harvest House team, for gracing me through these years we've partnered together. To Bob Hawkins Sr., for the vision of writing books. To Gene Skinner, for impeccable editing of all my books at Harvest House. To Christianne Debysingh, for the privilege of sharing in an amazing display of grace during the time I was writing this book. To Bob Hawkins Jr., Terry Glaspey, and LaRae Weikert, for sharing your grace with me every time we meet and dream about books that will change lives for Christ.

CONTENTS

Grow in the grace and knowledge of our Lord
and Savior Jesus Christ. To Him be the glory,
both now and to the day of eternity. Amen.

2 Peter 3:18

✳

Return, O wanderer, now return,
And seek thy Father's face;
Those new desires which in thee burn
Were kindled by His grace.
Return, O wanderer, now return,
and wipe the falling tear:
Thy Father calls—no longer mourn;
'Tis love invites thee near.

William Benco Collyer

FOREWORD

Grace. We talk about it, marvel at it, and say we have it because of Jesus. But do we experience it, benefit from it, or actually *live* in it every single day? Perhaps the most fundamental—and least experienced—benefit of Jesus' finished work is this mystery of grace.

My friend Catherine knows this grace. I love what she writes: "When we receive Christ, we are forever under grace...the fulfillment of the New Covenant of grace never depends on us, only on God." What a staggering reality! Such freedom! Such extravagant love! Grace is received, not earned; bestowed, not achieved. We can finally stop striving and performing and start thriving and enjoying.

I yearn to walk confidently in God's grace, don't you?

In this beautiful book Catherine takes us on the grace walk our hearts are longing for. "The more I realized the truth about grace," she writes, "the more I experienced true freedom in life."

As you read these pages, I'm certain your tentative steps will become more confident and joyful as you boldly walk into grace.

Nancy Stafford
actress, author, and popular speaker

INTRODUCTION

Do you remember the first time you traveled to a new place, a distant land that was quite unlike the place you knew as home? You packed your bags, your heart raced with excitement, and you trembled with a bit of fear and anticipation. What would you encounter on your journey? Would you even enjoy your destination?

When I became a Christian, I had no idea what had happened to me, and I certainly was unaware of the adventure ahead. The most unanticipated facet of my journey with God may be summed up in one small word with big meaning: *grace*. The world doesn't know about grace, and the church doesn't always prepare you for grace. Why? Because there is very little experience of grace in the world and precious little understanding of it in the church. The definition of grace is difficult to articulate in words.

Earlier this year I met with my friend Ney Bailey, an author and lover of God. We were talking about what it means to know God. She stopped in the midst of our conversation, turned to me, grabbing my full attention, and said, "Catherine, do you know what book I think you should write next?"

"What book, Ney?" I asked.

"I think you should write about grace. People don't experience grace.

They don't know it. I think grace is so important for us to understand and experience in our lives."

My eyes widened. "Ney, you're not going to believe this, but guess what—grace *is* my next book! I've already begun studying and writing. God's grace is one of the most powerful aspects of my life."

Ney and I just looked at each other and smiled. We knew our conversation was one of those God-ordained moments where eternity touches the heart and humanity collides with God and His plans. God confirmed my assignment through Ney. I thought, *God, You must have an amazing adventure in store for all of us.*

And so, dear friend, I invite you to enter the land of grace. Grace is God's land, the place where He lives and works, and the terrain where He plants you and grows you into a mature, healthy, vibrant child of the King. Grace is behind, before, and surrounding every single gift you receive from God. So pack your bags, dear friend, for once you embark on God's grace adventure, there's no turning back. When you truly experience God's extravagant grace, everything you've known before pales in comparison, and you won't look behind you—only forward, on into eternity.

An Affirmation of Grace

Because of God's grace...

> I am secure, forgiven, accepted, and loved
> forever by God.
>
> I am always in God's audience, united with
> Christ, and indwelt by the Holy Spirit.
>
> I stand in extravagant grace, the perfect
> environment for spiritual growth.
>
> I am blessed with every spiritual blessing
> and have everything I need.
>
> I am God's beautiful masterpiece, designed
> for His purposes and plans.
>
> I have the hope of heaven, where I will
> live with Christ forever.

I believe it, receive it, and live it.

Part 1

THE GARDEN OF GRACE

1

In the Garden of Grace

She stood behind the open door, her eyes fixed on the English missionaries who had come to visit her in-laws. Hidden from view, she stared at their gentle faces and felt deep sobs welling up from a place inside she did not care to reveal, not even to herself. *No, I can't entertain the hope I see in these people. How could I have possibly arrived at such a despicable life, with no way of escape? Trapped in this house, forever doomed.* At 19, she was already a widow with a child—a most desperate position for any woman in India in the late 1800s.

Buried in her memories were earlier years of tender love from parents who regarded her as their greatest treasure, naming her Ponnamal, meaning "gold." Her parents showered her with every possible advantage, blessing their bright young daughter with a good education. Then, as was the custom, she was given in marriage to an older man. Clothed in silk, decorated with beautiful jewelry, high-spirited and gentle Ponnamal left the warmth of her father's house to marry a professor at the mission college. Her marriage brought disillusionment, but the birth of a child brought her joy. And then came the sudden, shocking death of her husband only a year after their wedding. Ponnamal had journeyed from safety to sorrow and now to despair. Widows were outcasts in India. What would she do? Where would she go?

19

"We'll take you in," responded her in-laws with disdain and resignation ringing in their voices. Ponnamal realized her place in their home. They never let her forget. "You're only here because of the child. No, you can't change your clothes. You're a widow. Only soiled things become you. No, you can't have a comb. You are no good. You're a burden on us. Even if you work all day, it won't be enough to repay all we have done for you."

At first Ponnamal thought, *Surely they don't know me. When they see how hard I work and how much I want to help, they'll be kind. They'll change.* But the more she tried, the worse her situation became. Sinking into despair, she began to believe their lies.

One night she thought, *I cannot endure my lot in life. I hear the well calling me as it has called others in the past. I can end my suffering with death.* She waited for her mother-in-law to fall asleep and then grasped the door's iron bolts and slipped out into the darkness of the night. She felt relieved to escape as the open air and vast starry sky soothed her heart. She stood by the well, ready to throw herself over the edge.

But then she remembered something she had read long ago. *Wasn't there an Indian widow who actually accomplished a great deed for her country? I know I read that somewhere. If she could accomplish something worthwhile, then why can't I do the same? Maybe there is hope for me yet.* Fleeting excitement simmered within and drove her back to her bed, where she lay for hours, thinking wishful thoughts until dawn.

The next morning her eyes sparkled with anticipation of unknown adventure. And now, only days later, standing behind a door, invisible to all but God, she listened intently to Mr. and Mrs. Walker, missionaries committed to sharing Jesus with others in India. They asked about the wild-eyed young girl they had noticed. "Who is the young woman living with you?"

"She is the widow of our son," replied Ponnamal's in-laws.

"We'd like to invite all of you to attend church," replied the Walkers.

Surprisingly, Ponnamal was allowed to attend church on Sundays.

The preacher gave deep, vibrant, Spirit-filled messages with rapid sentences in the complicated Tamil language. He may have thought only the men were understanding and hearing the message. But Ponnamal discerned the meaning of those words better than all others in attendance. *This Jesus is the one I have been longing for all my life. I never have to feel alone again.* Transformed, Ponnamal entered into new life in Christ and was filled with a supernatural joy and peace. Outwardly, she endured the same trapped, hopeless existence, but with newfound serenity, she performed the drudgery of duties in a strength and triumph no amount of reproach could weaken.

One day, Mrs. Walker, with characteristic gentleness, asked, "Could Ponnamal stay an extra hour after the Sunday service to teach Sunday school?"

Again, surprisingly, her father-in-law responded, "Yes, she may."

Ponnamal excitedly thought, *I can hardly believe I have this open door. But I will walk through it.* And walk through it she did, teaching women of all ages.

Ponnamal was teaching one Sunday when she noticed a slight, gentle-faced, dark-haired English woman watching her. *I wonder who she is? She seems like someone with whom I could pour out my soul.*

The English woman watched Ponnamal teach and thought, *What strikes me is her power over them. There is something quite unusual about her. Ponnamal is a woman set apart.* Later that morning, the woman walked up to her and said, "I'm Amy Carmichael." Ponnamal could have never guessed how one meeting would alter the course of her life.

Amy intently watched Ponnamal's in-laws at church. One Sunday, she saw the father-in-law crush a butterfly against the church wall during the service. She thought with disgust, *How symbolic the crushing of that insect seems. The only one he has within his power to crush is Ponnamal.* Amy began wondering, *What can I do?* and then *What must I do?*

Amy knocked on the in-laws' door, determined in her purpose. Winsomely, knowingly, she approached in the way God had shown her, finally asking permission for Ponammal to come with her for just one afternoon. "I would like Ponnamal to accompany me on visits out on the mission field."

The father-in-law assured her, "Name the afternoon, and she may go."

Ponnamal, on hearing those words, felt the prison doors open. *This is the day of Jubilee for me. Life will never be the same.* And she was right.

When Amy arrived at the in-laws' house, she scanned Ponnamal's face, looking into eager yet powerfully controlled eyes intent on answering God's call. Amy thought, *Yes, Ponnamal, we will serve the Lord together in His love and power.* Together they walked out of that oppressive house into an afternoon of service for the Lord.

Some time later, Amy boldly asked the in-laws, "I would like Ponnamal to join me in ministry and travel throughout India, serving the Lord." Miraculously, they agreed. Thus began the adventures of Amy Carmichael and Ponnamal, coworkers in the missionary work of Dohnavur Fellowship in India.

✳

In Ponnamal's story we see a tremendous rescue and restoration of a soul. What made her rescue possible? Grace—God's pure and powerful grace. Ponnamal was helpless, unable to save herself in her life situation. She seemed to be doomed to a life of drudgery and despair. Then, amazingly, she experienced spiritual transformation. She was given a life of ministry with one of the greatest missionaries of all time. Grace benefits the least likely and showers the unfortunate with unimaginable gifts, producing results that are almost too good to be true. God, because of His grace, finds invisible people and pours out His gifts of grace: new identity, beauty, strength, provision, new life, forgiveness of sins, and more. Ponnamal received the touch of God's grace and lived forever after in its warm embrace. And you and I must do the same.

Grace is seemingly a mystery. To many, grace is a theological term, not an experiential reality. When asked to define it, most cannot find adequate words. But you and I need the grace of God. Without God's grace we cannot be saved, thrive, grow, or live. We depend on God's grace every waking moment. More often than we care to admit, we don't realize the miraculous work and wonder of God's grace.

A number of years ago, during a busy time of ministry, I remarked to myself, *I want to grow deeper in my relationship with God. I wonder what God wants to do in my life?* A phrase came to mind then that I could not stop thinking about: *Grow in the grace...* I thought, *That must be part of a verse in the Bible, but I have no idea where it is.* Finally, when I dimly began to wonder if God might be trying to speak to my heart, I pulled out my trusty concordance to see if I could find it. Sure enough, I found 2 Peter 3:18: "Grow in the grace and knowledge of our Lord and Savior Jesus Christ. To Him be the glory, both now and to the day of eternity. Amen." I read that verse as though for the first time. Although I had not yet plumbed the depths of it, I felt I had discovered one of God's secrets in the Bible, a truth reserved for those who will open the pages of His Word and regard seriously what He says. I knew the secret was related to grace, but I also knew I couldn't give a good definition beyond what I'd heard others say about it.

Since my college years, I've known grace as God's Riches At Christ's Expense. This acronym helps me remember part of what God's grace does for me, but I wanted to know more. What is grace, really? And more importantly, how relevant is grace to me? Why do I need grace, and how can I get it? So I began living in this one simple verse, thinking about its meaning for my own life with the Lord.

The lessons I've been learning about growing in the garden of grace and receiving God's gifts of grace form the substance of this book. Grace grabbed my heart and enlarged it, enabling me to powerfully experience more of the presence and person of God Himself. The more I realized the truth about grace, the more I experienced true freedom in life. What Jesus says is true—the truth will make you free (John

8:32). More than anything, we need to know the truth about grace, for grace unlocks the door to blessed freedom in Christ.

Grace is the free, unmerited favor of God. You can't earn it. You don't deserve it. Grace is at the heart of all God does toward you, for you, and in you. Grace finds you, saves you, and keeps you. Grace gives you everything you need, more than you could ever want, and places you in an eternal, secure, favorable position forever. You stand in grace, according to Paul the apostle (Romans 5:2).

A.W. Tozer writes in *The Knowledge of the Holy* that grace is the "good pleasure of God that inclines Him to bestow benefits upon the undeserving."[1] Chuck Swindoll, in his book *The Grace Awakening*, points out that "God helps the helpless, the undeserving, those who don't measure up, those who fail to achieve the standard."[2]

The foundation of grace is the New Covenant, an unchanging, binding agreement made by God, ratified by the blood of Christ, and guaranteed by promises that can never be broken (Hebrews 8:7-13). The Old Covenant was based on the law, which could be broken (James 2:10). When we receive Christ, we are forever under grace (Romans 6:14), and our future is secure, for the covenant can *never* be broken because Christ guarantees its fulfillment. The fulfillment of the New Covenant of grace never depends on us, only on God.

The apostle Paul is the perfect New Testament expositor of the grace (Greek, *charis*) of God, for he knew grace perhaps better than most in the first-century church. He was a Pharisee and knew the finer points of God's law. He hated the church and persecuted those who loved and followed Christ. And yet Jesus met him on the Damascus road, loved him, saved him, forgave him, and gave him everlasting life. Paul knew he did not deserve salvation, yet he could not deny his experience on the road to Damascus that day. He met Jesus. He personally knew the manifold grace of God. *Grace* became one of Paul's favorite words. In fact, he loved describing grace with additional words like *much more* grace, *abundant* grace, *superabundant* grace, *abounding* grace, *reigning* grace, *exceeding* grace, *exceeding abundant* grace, *glorious* grace, and *sufficient* grace.

John Newton, the slave trader turned preacher, joined in Paul's practice of elaborating on God's grace gift. For Newton, the free, unmerited favor of God was "Amazing Grace." And grace is amazing! Here's why. Paul explained that salvation is not possible any other way but by grace through faith (Ephesians 2:8). Again, you can't earn what God freely gives. You can only receive God's grace-filled gift. Paul referred to "the surpassing riches of His grace in kindness toward us in Christ Jesus" (Ephesians 2:7). Throughout the New Testament, Paul constantly attached grace to every aspect of our experience with God.

The effects of God's grace in our lives are endless. Joseph Cooke, in his book *Celebration of Grace,* describes grace as "nothing more or less than the face that love wears when it meets imperfection, weakness, failure, sin. Grace is what love is and does when it meets the sinful and the undeserving."[3] Donald Grey Barnhouse, a twentieth-century expositor and preacher, explained the relationship between God's unmerited favor and love when he said, "Love that goes upward is worship; love that goes outward is affection; love that stoops is grace."

I like to think of grace as God's love in action. When you think of grace, think of God's arms open wide to you, regardless of what you have done. Grace opens the floodgates and allows God's endless love to pour into our lives, moment by moment, on into eternity. You have grace for today, grace for tomorrow, and grace forever. Now *that's* an extravagant, outrageous grace. Cathleen Falsani, in her book *Sin Boldly,* describes grace as "audacious, unwarranted, and unlimited."[4]

At the heart of grace is a gift. I recently read a friend's Facebook page, and he mentioned his own thankfulness for his son's recent university scholarship. He wrote, "We are thankful to God, for it is a gift of grace." My friend earned a doctoral degree in theology at Dallas Theological Seminary, so his words are highly credible. He understands, in the deepest theological sense from God's Word, that everything we receive from God is a gift of His grace. God gives and gives and gives some more. His gifts are the overflow of His grace because giving is what grace does. In understanding grace, we need to imagine a huge box wrapped in a big beautiful bow. And when we pull the bow off and unwrap the gift, we find infinite, unending riches from God.

The greatest gift the God of all grace gave you is Christ, who is full of grace. Brian Edwards says, "Grace is not merely God's attitude towards undeserving rebels, it is ultimately and above all God giving himself to us and for us—as the Man on a cross."[5] Christ's death on the cross opens the floodgates of grace in your life. He died in your place, paid the penalty for your sin, and cleared the way for you to live with Him forever. In Christ, you are given manifold grace, riches, and an eternal inheritance. When you believe and receive God's grace, you realize the best news imaginable is true—you are no longer alienated from God, but accepted and loved by Him forever.

The power of grace in our lives is seen in Peter's words, "Grow in the grace..." That little word *in* points to the place where we truly live once we enter into a life-changing relationship with Jesus. It's one thing to believe grace or even receive grace. But it is quite another thing to live in grace. Living in grace means being planted in the environment, breathing in the air, and thriving in the atmosphere of grace. Grace is like a beautiful garden where we may grow and flourish.

When I was a little girl, I enjoyed walking in my grandmother's garden. My grandmother would spend many hours in her garden, caring for the flowers and vegetables she had planted. And so it is in the garden of grace. There in God's wondrous garden, we meet with the Lord Himself and receive from Him everything we need for renewal and restoration. The garden of God's grace is a place of security, abundance, provision, joy, and hope. Grace gives you what you need when you need it. Grace can make you grow into the woman God wants you to be.

God is the God of all grace. He wants to shower you with every grace-filled gift you need to grow—His provision for your needs, His perspective for your circumstances, and His presence for your journey from time to eternity. And so the most important aspect of grace is learning to receive all the gifts God's grace-filled heart gives you. In fact, we are actually stewards of grace, which means we are entrusted with the responsibility of receiving and sharing God's gracious gifts (1 Peter 4:10).

We often struggle to believe God's grace is really extended toward us. We think, *No, God can't really love me. Not after all I've done.* I think about the day I first surrendered my life to the Lord. I immediately remarked to my college roommate, "How can God possibly forgive me?" God's grace is usually a surprise for the sinner, an undeserved gift waiting to be unwrapped and enjoyed.

We are trained to earn what we have. And if an undeserved, unmerited gift is given to us, we often turn it down, reeling from the sting of our own guilt and pain. Many spend their lifetimes trying to earn or pay for what God has already given by His manifold grace. Many are pursuing something they believe is elusive, trying desperately to find God. What an eye-opening day when we discover that God is the initiator who seeks us out and extends the gift of His grace.

In God's land of grace, we discover grace is received, not earned. David Jeremiah describes the discovery of the intoxicating light of grace as "finding a knothole in the high gates of heaven."[6] Grace washes away our guilt and shame and gives us forgiveness and eternal life. Eventually, God's grace opens our eyes to our future and a blessed hope. Most importantly, we experience God's plan and purpose in our lives when we recognize, receive, and enjoy the gifts God gives us out of His heart of grace. And so, let's resolve together that we will no longer try to earn or work for God's grace. Instead, *believe it,* knowing that what God says is truer than what we feel. *Receive it,* daily unwrapping God's abundant gifts of grace. And *live it*—growing deep and thriving in God's garden of grace.

✳

A young man grew tired of living at home. When would his father die so he could receive his inheritance? All he could think about was the money he would receive and the freedom such wealth would afford. Finally, he could wait no longer. "Father, give me my share of what will come to me at your death," he demanded.

Such a request was insulting, and the father could rightly have chosen out of anger to disown the son. But then he would have no hope of reconciliation. And so the father, with a broken heart, said, "Here is your portion." His older brother clearly resented his brother's actions and responded with silence.

Normally the eldest son would step in and plead with a rebellious brother on behalf of the father. He would remind the young man of the father's love. But in this case, the older brother could say nothing, for he was in rebellion of another kind. And so the father's heart ached for two lost sons. They both rejected their father's grace, mercy, and love.

The younger son took his inheritance and left town in a hurry, not wishing to face the scorn of the entire community because of his actions. *I'm out of here. Now I'm free to do what I want!* he may have thought. He left his own country for a foreign land.

In a short time, he squandered all his money. *Now what will I do? I can't go home. My brother hates me. And I cannot endure the reproach of the people in my village because of what I've done to my father. And I have insulted my father, so he has surely disowned me.* The young man's bad situation worsened, and he became desperate because of the famine in the land. *I'm starving. I've got to find something to eat! I'll see if I can hire on with one of the wealthy landowners here in this country.*

The landowner looked at this beggar asking for work. *Who does this young man think he is? I know how to get rid of him—I'll offer him a job he would never even consider. I'll let him feed the pigs.*

"I'll take it!" replied the desperate young man. As he offered the food to the pigs, he thought, *I wish I could stomach what these swine are eating. I'm so hungry. Even the pigs eat better than me. There is no mercy for me. Not a drop of kindness from anyone. Only disgust.*

Suddenly, in his weakened state, he came to his senses with a new thought. *What am I doing? Even my father's hired hands eat better than this. I can earn my way and eat enough by hiring on with my own father as one of his hired hands.* He planned his words carefully. *I'll say, "I have sinned against heaven and in your sight; I am no longer worthy to be called your son; make me as one of your hired men." Yes, that will work,* he thought as he began the long journey home.

The young man fully expected reproach from the community and a long wait before he would be granted an audience with an angry, estranged father. What the young man had not counted on was his father's heart. He thought his father was like all people. He didn't yet know his father was unlike all others in the world. His father did outrageous, out-of-this-world things because of one quality—extravagant grace.

Walking on the dusty road, approaching town, the young son grew more fearful, dreading the impending confrontation. *What will happen when I enter the village?* he thought. His head was down, his eyes on his feet as he trudged along.

But then he looked up. *What is this? Who are these people running toward me?* And then his heart lifted. What he saw was more than he could bring himself to believe. *Could it be? No way—but it is! My father! Running toward me with his arms wide open!*

The father, setting aside the cultural rights of estrangement and throwing himself into one act of humiliation, left the comfort of his home and raced out to receive the young man, not as a hired hand, but as his beloved son. The father would have nothing less than the very best for his recovered child. He paid the price of humiliation and loss of face and raced out to his son, thus settling forever in front of the entire town the nature of their relationship and full reconciliation.

Stunned by the outpouring of his father's love, the young son said, "Father, I have sinned against heaven, and in your sight; I am no longer worthy to be called your son." Now he knew, as never before, what he had in his father—the relationship, the love, the grace, and the greatness of his father. *How could I have been so ignorant of my father's great love for me?*

The father gave him no time for further thought. "Quickly bring out the best robe and put it on him, and put a ring on his hand and sandals on his feet; and bring the fattened calf, kill it, and let us eat and celebrate." The father restored their relationship in the presence of all. The robe signified restoration to sonship, the ring entrusted him with power, and the shoes symbolized his rank as a son, not a servant. Only the father could restore these things through his own gracious favor. The result of extravagant grace was reconciliation between father and son and the fulfillment of the father's steadfast, unchanging desire.

But the father had yet another son who needed his grace. This son had troubles of a different kind. He did not know his father's love any better than the son who left home. The older son had rejected the father in perhaps a deeper way, having refused intimate fellowship while living in the same house. Equally estranged, he was aloof and distant from the father. He didn't understand that he had broken his father's heart as much as the younger son had. Standing outside the house, the older son asked one of the young servants, "What is going on? Why is there music and dancing?"

The servant quickly responded with excitement. "Your brother has come, and your father has killed the fattened calf because he has received him back safe and sound."

"Of course! Typical. My father throws a party for a worthless son but has never thrown one celebration for me. What has he ever done for me? I have done everything right and yet received nothing for it. I'm infuriated that my father wouldn't make such a terrible son pay for all he has done against the family."

Standing outside the house, the older son's anger rose to a boiling point. He refused to enter the house or engage in the celebration. In their culture, his aloofness and absence from the party would have been considered an insult to the father and the guests. Once again, the father could have chosen to reject and disown a rebellious son. But again, he responded with extravagant and outrageous grace.

Just as the son was thinking about the celebration, he looked up to find himself face-to-face with his father. Not afraid to lose face with his guests and suffer the humiliation of lowering himself to quell unjust rebellion, the father left the party to reach out to his son.

When the older son saw the father, he became more obstinate. "Look! I've been serving you for a long time, and I've done everything you told me to. It's not fair. Your younger son doesn't deserve the party—I do. But you've never thrown a party for me!"

The father loved this son and wanted him for his own, not estranged, but in fellowship. And so he did what no other would do. He did not walk away, but reached out in grace-filled love. "Son, you have always been with me, and all that is mine is yours. But we had to celebrate and rejoice, for this brother of yours was dead and has begun to live and was lost and has been found."

How did the older son respond? What did he say to such grace offered in the face of callous hatred?

☀

A hush most likely moved across the crowd of listeners, and palpable tension may have filled the air when Jesus told this story. Through the windows and rooms of every detail and character, hard-hearted Pharisees were encouraged to see themselves and others anew—with eyes of grace. Jesus invited them to enter into a relationship with God and share His heart of love expressed in grace-covered actions. When He heard them say, "This man receives sinners and eats with them," He was compelled to show them God's magnificent grace through the art of a pointed, passionate story. He gave them this parable of the prodigal son, a beloved tale of hope for every sinner saved by grace.

But really, this grace story encompasses two sons who desperately needed God's unconditional love and unmerited favor. Both were in a hopeless state, unable to help themselves in any way, completely reliant on their father's mercy. We know the rest of the story for the younger son. But what about the end result for the older son? That part of the story is unfinished. God seems to leave all who listen, including the Pharisees of Jesus' day, with a question: "Will you set aside your prejudices, resentments, sins, despair, and despondency, and step into the garden of My grace? Live here in My grace and share in My heart of love."

The highlight of Jesus' story, looming larger than any of the details, is the father's heart. His actions were unexpected, nothing like human responses to sin and rebellion. And that was His point. God seemingly says to us at every turn, "Know Me. Understand My heart. I love you and want you in close relationship with Me." He wants us to know Him not as we *think* He is or *want* Him to be, but as He *really* is. He is always more than we think He is and more than we know Him to be. There is always more to know of God and His infinite, eternal, magnificent grace.

God's grace is outrageous and a huge surprise for all who receive it. We can relate to the younger son, who squandered opportunities and needed forgiveness for willful sin. Sometimes we are like the older son, caught up in pride and arrogance, stepping out of the grateful appreciation of God's grace-covered gifts in our lives. Often, we don't even realize God's grace and mercy acting on our behalf because we are so focused on ourselves. Through a poignant word-woven picture, Jesus extends the invitation to enter into the land of grace and enjoy an intimate relationship with the Father.

Jesus shows us the Father's heart. If you want to know what God is like, just look at Jesus, for He explains God (John 1:18). The more you watch Jesus in relationship with others in the Gospels, the greater you will realize, experience, and understand His grace.

Jesus, in telling the parable of the prodigal son, confronts legalism with love and grace. We can know by looking at Jesus that we cannot earn favor; we can only receive His grace. We can receive God's grace because Jesus died in our place on the cross, receiving the full penalty for every one of our sins. His death was enough for every sin.

Legalism places the burden of performance on man, not God. But if we could do anything to earn God's love and acceptance, then Jesus died needlessly on the cross. Bill Bright used to say that legalism is the greatest heresy of Christianity. You can't earn God's favor or love, but you can receive it. Stepping off of the performance treadmill is a challenge for any child of God. And sometimes, even in the church, grace is a missing element. There are always those who pull you into a legalistic way of approaching God. Philip Yancey says, "Oddly, I sometimes find a shortage of grace within the church, an institution founded to proclaim, in Paul's phrase, 'the gospel of grace.'"[7]

✳

I grew up wanting desperately to be accepted by my classmates in grade school. Without a doubt, I was one of the great people pleasers of all time. I would often think, *If only I have the right clothes and get the best grades, I will be part of the in crowd.* Meeting Jesus changed my whole approach to life because I became assured of His love and acceptance. He pulled me into a whole new environment with Him—the garden of grace. And living in the grace garden, breathing its atmosphere, walking and talking with Him, I realized God loves to bestow gifts of grace on undeserving sinners. His love changes us as He transforms us on the inside, makes us beautiful, provides for our needs, and sets us free to love, worship, and serve Him. In the garden of grace, we find ourselves in the perfect environment to thrive and grow.

Have you ever traveled to another country? I remember my first trip to Europe. My husband chose Italy for our destination. I thought, *Oh, I can't wait to get off the plane and visit this new place I've heard about but never seen!* I studied books about Italy and learned about various tourist attractions. But nothing prepared me for that first moment when we boarded the vaporetto (a boat) and traveled on the water to the Hotel Danieli in Venice. I had never been to a place where people traveled by boat to reach their destination. With time in Italy, I grew familiar with the ways of the people and their customs, and I even learned some of their language.

The garden of grace is like a new country, a place unlike any you have known before. We need to learn the ways and language of grace because grace has a unique vocabulary unlike what you will hear in the world. Here's how Joseph Cooke describes it:

> Grace is not the kind of thing that you can study once, and then conclude that you have it nailed down…Grace needs to permeate deeper and deeper and deeper into our minds, attitudes, feelings, relationships, behavior, service for God and others. It needs to go on and on changing us. It needs to become an ever more vital, motivating force in our lives.[8]

You can always spot those who know life in the garden of grace, for they act with unusual mercy and love, and they speak out of kindness and compassion rather than resentment and vengeance. They are selfless and are filled with loving, compassionate actions. And those who have never known grace are touched and moved by it. And if their hearts are open, they are changed forever.

One day while D.L. Moody was preaching, a homeless man, starving and bitterly cold, wandered into the meeting room. Moody's message that day encompassed the grace of God. Afterward, the man walked up to Moody and said, "I didn't come to hear you. I came to get warm. But my heart is broken. Do you think the grace of God can save me—a poor, miserable, vile wretch like me?"

Moody assured him, "Yes, definitely!" Moody later remarked, "It was refreshing to preach the gospel of the Son of God to that poor man."

Moody prayed with the man and found him a place to stay for the night. But Moody didn't stop there, for grace gives and gives and then gives some more. The next day, Moody arranged for someone to retrieve the man's coat from the pawnshop. This man, without a hope in the world, wandered into a warm meeting hall for protection and found the secure love of Jesus in the garden of God's grace.

Moody, one of the greatest evangelists of the nineteenth and twentieth centuries, influenced thousands of men and women and understood grace better than most people. He used to tell his audiences, "I have had more trouble with myself than with any other man I've met."

Ponnamal certainly discovered the power of God's grace when God found her tucked away in a far corner of India. Who could have guessed that God would give her the gift of ministry with Amy Carmichael? And the story of God's grace continues through your life and mine.

Friend, as I write these words, I wonder if you have discovered the magnificence of life in the garden of God's grace? Do you hear God's invitation to come and live in His garden? Do you know His love and acceptance as a reality in your own life? Do you realize you can do nothing to earn His favor? If so, it's time to throw a party for those who are lost have been found. And the adventure has only just begun. Let's step into the garden and discover the lifelong, always-new, incredible experience of growing in God's amazing grace.

GROW DEEP IN THE GARDEN OF GRACE

She heard the door close, seemingly with finality. Intentionally she did not look back. *I'm free.* Then she turned her gaze to Amy and wondered, *What is ahead for all of us? Whatever it is, I can't wait!* And so Ponnamal joined Amy's group of itinerant ministers of the gospel, a band of women and girls dedicated to reaching other women for Christ in India. Amy explained, "Our work is pioneer work, not work in prepared ground. In some places they've never seen someone like me. We must look for any sign of welcome, an open door whereby we may reach women with the gospel of Christ."

"What do you want me to do?" asked Ponnamal.

"You will preach, along with me, in the marketplaces. And sometimes you will give a message at the village churches."

"I'm afraid. What if no one listens? What if I can't find the right words?"

"The Lord will give you the words when you need them. And in some places, people won't respond as we would like. We must be faithful and leave the results to God," replied Amy.

I have much to learn, thought Ponnamal.

Ponnamal especially loved the mornings in this new life God had given her. After breakfast, through the hottest part of the day, she joined the other women in a study circle. Together they studied the Word of God. *I'm going to write down everything I learn as we read the Bible together. Later, I can study my notes and grow in my faith.*

Ponnamal could never have guessed how her study of God's Word would impact the lives of others. One day, one of the Tamil Bible students asked, "Ponnamal, may I copy your notes so I can learn also?"

"Of course," Ponnamal replied. Ponnamal's notes from the study circle became the talk of the Tamil Bible students. They copied everything Ponnamal wrote and passed the lessons to others. The study circle was the beginning of God's ordained spiritual growth plan for Ponnamal.

One day, as this small band of women traveled from village to village, Amy spotted an opportunity to tell others about Jesus. But this time she said, "Ponnamal, let's give these people something to think about. Let's tell them what Jesus has done for them. It's your turn to stand up and give a message."

By now, Ponnamal was accustomed to the unusual challenges from her bold and courageous mentor. And so Ponnamal stepped into an open area next to one of the vendors in the marketplace and spoke from truths she had written from the Bible readings in the study circle. "Jesus died for you. Do you know what that means? He loves you and desires a relationship with you."

Soon a crowd gathered. Some listened. Others asked questions. "What do you mean? Tell us about Jesus."

Ponnamal discovered something new in stepping beyond her comfort zone, *The Lord gives me strength. And I am so different now in my new life.*

Ponnamal was not the same fearful and cowering woman who left her in-laws' house. Amy Carmichael described Ponnamal during their years in ministry as one "who had developed a gift of fine and forceful speech, and could hold a turbulent open-air meeting in a big busy market" and "was an immense help always."

Ponnamal grew quickly in her new grace-filled environment. Amy noted that Ponnamal "proved herself a delightful companion; it was good to see the timid look passing from her, as she began to realize her liberty." Their little itinerant band of women was the first of its kind in that part of India, and they relied on the Lord to strengthen them for the work.

✳

Ponnamal experienced what every believer in Christ is designed to experience—spiritual growth. When Jesus invites you to step into the garden of His grace, He intends to grow you into a mature Christian, a spiritual giant of the faith, one who stands strong, clings to Christ, and follows Him wherever He leads.

When I graduated from seminary, my husband took me on a trip to Yosemite National Park. I'll never forget the day he said, "Catherine, today you're going to see something that will amaze you—the giant redwood trees. Just looking at them increases your faith in God because of their immense size and design." I couldn't wait. We drove to the Mariposa Grove of Giant Sequoias. The size of these redwood trees was unbelievable. These are some of the largest trees in the world. The tallest redwoods can reach 350 feet—higher than the Statue of Liberty—and are larger in circumference than a Greyhound bus. And some are at least 2000 years old. They were alive when Jesus walked this earth! But growing something much smaller, like a squash, takes a lot less time—only a few months.

God is making us tall, like a giant redwood tree, not small, like a squash. And so our spiritual growth will take time. Jeremiah 17:7-8 and Psalm 1 liken our lives to a tree planted by a powerful stream, with roots reaching deep down into the rich nutrients of the moist soil. The growth of the tree enables it to withstand drought and heat and to produce fruit through every season of its life. This picture of a tree helps us understand that we are not meant to stay in one place spiritually, but to grow. And we are to grow tall, like the giant redwood trees, becoming spiritual giants in the kingdom of God.

✳

The phone rang. It was my brother, Robert. "Cath, we're having the baby. You need to come, right away."

"I'll be there, Rob. Just have to pack my bags."

"Oh Cath…I can't believe I'm going to be a father."

"I know, Rob—it's so exciting! I'll see you soon."

I threw my bags in the car and flew down the road, making the four-hour drive in record time. I drove straight to the hospital and asked for directions to the maternity ward. *I'm going to have a little niece. I cannot believe my brother is going to be the father of a little girl.*

Finally, I turned the corner, following my brother's voice behind the closed door of the hospital room. Just as I arrived, the door opened, and there was my brother, holding a baby girl wrapped in a yellow blanket. To this day, I cannot find words to describe his face—maybe *sheer love* comes close. Smiling, he said, "Catherine, meet Kayla." He pulled back the blanket to reveal the most precious face I've ever seen, eyes sparkling with intelligence even though she was less than a day old. Of course, I am slightly biased, but I do think our Kayla is still the most brilliant little girl in the world. Then Rob said, "Cath, do you want to hold her?"

"Oh Rob, yes, I would love to hold her."

"Sit over in that rocking chair, and I'll hand her to you."

I looked over to the chair and thought, "Imagine that—a rocking chair in a maternity ward. Good idea!"

I sat down and held out my arms. "Here she is, Cath."

Holding her and looking into her face, I began to cry. And pray. *Lord, I pray for this little girl, that she will be Your woman in the world. That she will grow strong in You, shine brightly with Your glory, and live for You.*

Then I began talking to her. "Kayla, you are beautiful. Do you know how incredibly excited your aunt is to hold you now? Do you know how much I love you?" Of course, Kayla just looked into my face with an expression of wonder and curiosity. She had no idea what I was saying to her.

That first day in the hospital was the beginning of our adventures with Kayla. Every time I visited Phoenix, I would pick up my little Kayla and hold her close. She would cling tightly to me, so very dependent on my strength and provision.

Soon Kayla was able to crawl, and life became even more exciting in her world. You never knew where Kayla might end up, and we had to watch her every single moment. Her discovery of the outside world on her first journey in a stroller was one of the most hilarious sights you could imagine. As her parents pushed her in the stroller along the neighborhood sidewalk, she squealed with delight, arms outstretched, at nothing in particular. Just the experience of it brought delight to her soul.

Watching Kayla grow has been amazing and wonderful and has helped me understand God's perspective of our spiritual growth. She is certainly more than she was when I held her in my arms for the first time eight years ago. As she has grown from a newborn baby to a young girl, our relationship has become more than it was before. Our times together are filled with deep conversations about life, God, and family. We love talking about ideas. Kayla is one of the deepest thinkers I've ever known. I love watching her grow, and I so enjoy participating in the process.

✳

The day I found 2 Peter 3:18 was so profound for me. The most significant word for me was *grace*. When God says, "Grow in the grace…" He is saying that grace is the environment where He has placed us so we can grow. Grace is like a garden that has everything we need to become the women He wants us to be. Just think how perfect God's garden of grace is for growth! Grace gives us security, for our future is certain—we have eternal life (Romans 6:14-23). Grace gives us a steadfast foundation—we stand in grace, forgiven of every sin (Romans 5:2). Grace gives us an abundance of every good gift—we have everything we need because of grace (Romans 5:17; 2 Corinthians 9:8).

Peter is the perfect one to give us this picture of the garden of grace as our growth environment. Perhaps no disciple of Jesus knew and appreciated God's grace as intimately as Peter. He and his brother Andrew began their careers as simple fishermen. One day, while casting their nets into the sea, Peter looked up and saw Jesus walking along the shore of the Sea of Galilee. *No one teaches like He does. His words seem to ask for a response from me. But what am I to do?* Just as Peter was thinking more deeply about Jesus, there He was, walking toward them. *He's coming this way. Good, I love talking with Him and listening to Him teach. No one is interested in me the way He is. Everything He says seems to be just for me.* This time, though, Peter noticed Jesus' approach was much more direct. He didn't seem to be looking for a crowd to teach; He was walking directly toward Peter. With purpose in His voice, He looked at Peter and his brother and said, "Follow Me, and I will make you fishers of men."

Peter didn't even stop to think about what those words might mean. Throwing his nets in the boat, he and Andrew waded to shore and ran to catch up to Jesus as He walked along the shore. Many fishermen were working on their trade that morning. And Jesus called two more to follow Him, James and John. Soon their number grew to 12. In time, Peter realized Jesus' true identity.

Jesus asked His small band of followers, "Who do you say that I am?"

Peter didn't even need to think about the answer. "You are the Christ, the Son of the living God." But what came next just astounded Peter, the simple fisherman.

"You are blessed, Peter, because flesh and blood did not reveal this to you, but My Father who is in heaven."

Peter may have thought, *What? God is revealing things to me?* He was no trained theologian. But he knew Jesus was more than a man. In a split second, he was able to confess the true identity of Jesus. *I've seen Him make paralyzed men walk, heal the blind, and feed five thousand people with just a few fragments of food. No mere man could perform such miracles.*

A feeling of invincible, unshakeable commitment to Jesus grew in Peter. Peter noticed a growing intensity of resolute movement toward something momentous in Jesus' attitude and words. He couldn't believe all he was hearing Jesus say on the night of Passover. "One of you will betray Me." And finally, he could no longer stay quiet when he heard Jesus say, "You will all fall away because of Me this night."

"Even though all may fall away because of You, I will never fall away," Peter insisted.

"Truly, I say to you that this very night, before a rooster crows, you will deny Me three times."

Three times I will deny You? thought Peter. "Even if I have to die with You, I will not deny You." All the disciples followed Peter's lead, insisting their devotion, even to death.

What happened next can be thought of as Peter's worst nightmare. He watched as the one he had grown to know and love was arrested by the chief priests and elders. *I'll protect Jesus. This can't happen!* Peter, no trained soldier but bold and courageous, pulled out his sword and cut off the ear of the chief priest's slave.

Jesus turned and said, "Put your sword away." Reaching over, Jesus touched and healed the ear of the slave.

Peter, shocked and confused, backed away. *He seems strange to me, on a mission I don't understand,* Peter may have thought. *I must see where they are taking Him.* Following at a distance, Peter saw the direction the group was headed. *Oh no, they're taking Him to Caiaphas, the high priest. I'll sit here in the courtyard with the officers and see what happens.*

While high drama was occurring between Jesus and Caiaphas, Peter experienced his own dark trial. A servant girl recognized him as a companion of Jesus. "You too were with Jesus the Galilean."

"I don't know what you are talking about."

Another servant girl said, "This man was with Jesus of Nazareth."

"I don't know the man."

Then some bystanders came and said to Peter, "Surely you too are one of them; for even the way you talk gives you away."

Peter, cursing and swearing, insisted, "I do not know the man!"

Immediately a rooster crowed.

The Lord turned and looked at Peter, His struggling disciple. Peter's eyes met his Lord's. The look of Jesus was embedded in his mind. Peter would never forget that moment of betrayal, when time seemed to stop. He stood and ran from the courtyard, bitter tears rolling down his face. The life he hoped for with his Lord was crushed forever in the darkness of his failure.

In the exciting early days, watching Jesus perform miracles, Peter could have never imagined the horrific events that would follow—the crucifixion of his beloved Master. The shock had been almost unbearable. But then the disciples' devastation had turned to amazement and joy. Jesus rose from the dead, and He appeared to them more than once. Still reeling from his failure, Peter had watched from a distance, perhaps believing he could never be close again.

One day, Peter told some of the other disciples, "I'm going fishing."

"We'll come with you," they said. They fished all night but caught nothing.

A man from shore called out to them, "Cast the net on the right-hand side of the boat, and you will find a catch." Following his advice, they caught more fish than they could haul in with their nets.

John turned to Peter. "It is the Lord."

Peter immediately put his outer garment on, jumped into the water, and swam to shore. He had to see Jesus. But before he could talk with Him, the other disciples arrived just in time to eat a breakfast prepared by the Lord. When they finished eating, Jesus spoke directly to Simon Peter, drawing him into intimate, personal conversation.

"Simon, son of John, do you love Me more than these?"

"Yes, Lord; You know that I love You."

"Tend My lambs."

Three times Jesus confirmed His calling of Peter as His servant, finally saying, "Follow Me!"

A shower of grace washed over Peter that day, confirming the Lord's forgiveness, acceptance, and purpose for him in ministry. The Lord chose Peter to lead the first-century church in spite of his great failure. Peter could speak of the environment of grace for spiritual growth because he knew God's unmerited favor firsthand in his own life. Jesus, through the words Peter wrote in his letter, wants you to know you have nothing to earn or prove in order to spiritually grow. You are in the garden of grace, and you have everything you need. So now it's time to grow.

✷

I sat in Leann's living room. I looked at the other college girls there and thought, *I wonder what we are going to do. I've said yes to being in Leann's action group, but now what?*

Leann, with her Bible open, said to all of us, "Welcome, everyone. I've invited you all together tonight because I want us to get to know one another better. You are all part of my action group. That means we are going to study God's Word together, grow together, and learn more about what it means to follow Christ."

I looked at the other girls and listened as they introduced themselves to the group. I thought, *These girls are so different from the girls I've known in the past. They seem friendly, like people I'd like to actually know better.* I had only recently surrendered my life to the Lord and was not used to spending time with Christians. So this whole adventure was new and exciting to me. Then Leann passed out a Bible study book called *The Christian and the Abundant Life.* I had never been in a Bible study. She explained that we would study this book week by week and then discuss what we learned together in our group. *I love this idea!* I thought.

I heard some of those involved in Campus Crusade use a term I had never known before. One of the women pointed to one of the Christian leaders and said, "She's a SWOG."

I asked, "What's a SWOG?"

"A Super Woman Of God."

I thought, *That's what I want to be—a super woman of God!*

Leann said, "Catherine, if you want to be a super woman of God, you must be serious about growing in your relationship with Christ. Your time alone with Him every day is vital. And studying God's Word will help you grow."

I experienced that first Bible study many years ago, but I remember the joy of it to this day. I discovered how much I love studying the Bible and growing in my walk with God. I've been in many Bible studies since then—Bible Study Fellowship, Precept Ministries groups, and others. Each study has signaled a new step in my spiritual growth.

When Peter invites us to "grow in the grace," what is he encouraging us to actually do? The word *grow* means to increase or add to something. In our case, growing means we become more than we are right now—more intimate with Christ, stronger in our faith, more enduring when we suffer, more fruitful in our walk with Jesus...more of everything the Bible encourages in our lives. Growth moves us from one place to another in our relationship with Jesus. We are not to stay stagnant in our walk with the Lord, but we are to "press on to maturity" (Hebrews 6:1). You are never too old to grow, and the mature Christian is always growing.

Spiritual growth is a process of God working in us to make us trophies of His grace so He can give a message of love and hope to the world. We are to grow up in all aspects into Christ (Ephesians 4:15). Our spiritual growth occurs within, but it affects every area of our lives and becomes outwardly apparent to anyone who is watching. We become more and more like Christ in everything we do. (See the rendering of Ephesians 4:15 in the New Living Translation.)

Dallas Willard, in his book *Renovation of the Heart,* explains how we grow more like Christ.

> Spiritual formation for the Christian basically refers to the
> Spirit-driven process of forming the inner world of the human
> self in such a way that it becomes the inner being of Christ
> himself...The result is that the "outer" life of the individual
> increasingly becomes a natural expression of the inner real-
> ity of Jesus and His teachings. Doing what he said and did
> increasingly becomes part of who we are.[1]

Paul alluded to a process in which Christ's life is formed in us (Galatians 4:19). Peter speaks of the following spiritual qualities that will
increase in our lives: faith, moral excellence, knowledge, self-control,
perseverance, godliness, kindness, and love (2 Peter 1:5-8). Alex Tang,
teacher at the Spiritual Formation Institute in Johor Bahru, Malay-
sia, describes the maturation process: "Spiritual formation is spiritual
growth. It is moving from being nourished by spiritual milk to spiritual meat. It is moving from breast-feeding...to a steak dinner."[2] We
are to become like giant redwood trees, tall enough to see forever, and
strong, with roots extending so deep that we receive the living water
of the Lord every moment of the day.

When I think of what it means to GROW, I think of Grace Reviving
Our Walk. Grace gives us everything we need to be revived, moment
by moment and day by day, as we are restored to God's plan and purpose for our lives. He gives us His Word, His indwelling Spirit, and
His abiding presence. When we draw near to Him, we are personally
and spiritually revived by Him. Through God's work in us, we spiritually grow. You will notice that the tree described in Jeremiah 17:7-8 is
able to thrive, grow, and bear fruit in spite of heat and drought. Spiritually growing Christians are undeterred by challenging situations, for
their roots reach deep into the life-giving provision of God Himself.
Spiritual growth is not what we do for God, but what God does in us.
That's why knowing life-transforming grace firsthand is so important
if we are to understand and experience spiritual growth.

Jesus likened our relationship with Him to a vine and branches, pointing out that He is our lifeblood. We grow and become fruitful only through our intimacy with Him (John 15:1-11). He says again and again, "Abide in Me," meaning that we are to remain in vital contact with Him. You cannot grow apart from Christ. In fact, Jesus said, "Apart from Me you can do nothing" (John 15:5). He may use others in your life to encourage you and teach you, but ultimately, you need to remain in vital contact with Christ and realize that the Lord is the one causing the growth (1 Corinthians 3:6-7).

Bill Hybels, pastor of Willow Creek Community Church, conducted a study a number of years ago measuring the effectiveness of their church in encouraging spiritual growth. The results were staggering. One in four members was either stalled in spiritual growth or dissatisfied with the church and thinking about leaving. Three important findings in the Willow Creek study point to key ingredients for spiritual growth:

1. Involvement in church activities does not necessarily determine spiritual growth.
2. Increasing intimacy with Christ results in spiritual growth.
3. Spiritual devotional disciplines lead to a Christ-centered life.[3]

Willow Creek also discovered four main categories of spiritual catalysts for spiritual growth: spiritual beliefs and attitudes, organized church activities, personal spiritual disciplines, and spiritual activities with others.[4]

When I first read the Willow Creek findings a number of years ago, I became very excited. You might be thinking, *What in the world is wrong with you, Catherine? Why would seemingly negative results encourage you?* Even Bill Hybels was ultimately thankful for those findings because dynamic change resulted, producing a greater impact in spiritual growth at Willow Creek and in hundreds of other churches. I was thrilled to know these spiritual growth discoveries because they simply confirmed my conviction of the importance of quiet time in our spiritual growth. I can say unequivocally that growing in my quiet time has led to development in all four of those Willow Creek spiritual catalyst categories and to my own spiritual growth.

When I decided early on that I wanted to be a SWOG and grow deep in my relationship with the Lord, I knew that the most important area of development was my quiet time, when I would remain in vital contact with Jesus. I discovered that my quiet time alone with the Lord was the key, the main secret for my spiritual growth in the garden of grace. In a quiet time, you abide (remain in vital contact) with Christ, renew your mind, revive your heart, and rest your soul. Your quiet time provides an environment for you to think about spiritual things, draw on God's power for daily living, and gain God's eternal perspective for your life.

You spend time with Christ in your quiet time. Think about this for a minute. Don't you become like the people you are with the most? Don't you learn the most from people who share the longest and best conversations with you? Quiet time is not a religious, tedious habit. Quiet time with God produces a vibrant, intimate, ongoing relationship with Him—what I like to call *radical intimacy*. Yes, you make an intentional choice every day to spend time with your Lord. And yes, the challenge of cultivating time with Him in a busy, fast-paced, driven culture requires planning and preparation. But the payoff of knowing Christ intimately because you have spent time with Him is unequalled by anything else you will ever do on earth.

A friend of mine recently asked me, "Cath, how do you convey the importance of a quiet time without putting a guilt trip on someone?"

I thought, *Great question!* I replied, "I focus on radical intimacy and *then* teach quiet time principles. The goal is knowing the Lord and living in the light of His smile." Life is a relationship with God, not a religious activity. Sometimes, when we feel guilty, however, our feelings may be pointing to a need for change, especially if we've chosen to squander our intimacy with God and have distanced ourselves from Him.

I recently spoke at a retreat for one of my favorite churches and women's ministries in the United States. After lunch on Saturday, I was given the rare opportunity to lead more than 500 women through one of my PRAYER quiet times. I had never thought of sharing such an intimate, personal experience with so many people. My quiet time is when I walk with my Lord in the garden of grace, when we share together in a one-on-one communication.

I grabbed my quiet-time basket and a cup of coffee, and I walked into the massive meeting room. There on the stage, a chair was waiting for me. I sat down, wired with a microphone, and set my quiet time basket next to me. I briefly spoke about setting aside a time and a place for daily quiet time and then shared the PRAYER quiet time plan:

> Prepare Your Heart
> Read and Study God's Word
> Adore God in Prayer
> Yield Yourself to God
> Enjoy His Presence
> Rest in His Love

Then I looked out into the faces of 500 eager women and said, "Let's spend some time together with the Lord." And I proceeded to lead them through a special quiet time experience with the Lord. (See our quiet time together in the appendix.)

I was surprised at the response I received from the women at that retreat. In less than an hour we had journeyed through a simple quiet time with the Lord. But for some, our time together was their first quiet time. Many shared with me that it was their favorite part of the weekend. Gazing through a window into someone else's quiet time communicates more than hearing ten messages about quiet time. And therein lies the difference between talking about quiet time and actually spending quiet time with the Lord. When you experience Him firsthand, you grow.

Quiet time with the Lord is really very simple. You connect with your Lord, draw near to Him in His Word, and talk with Him, sharing His heart. What makes quiet time different from any other time? Very simply, the Lord shows up. You don't see Him with your physical eyes, but you see and experience Him with the eyes of your heart. That's why Paul said, "I pray that the eyes of your heart may be enlightened, so that you will know what is the hope of His calling, what are the riches of the glory of His inheritance in the saints, and what is the surpassing greatness of His power toward us who believe" (Ephesians 1:18-19). When you spend quiet time with the Lord, you are drawn into His presence, where you receive your calling, discover how rich you are in Him, and experience the great power of the Holy Spirit. The more you learn from Him and the more you experience Him, the more you grow.

God's invitation to spiritual growth in grace is our pathway to becoming more than we are right now. We are works in progress, or WIPs, as I like to say. And WIPs need to remember that we are on a journey, an adventure of growth led by the Lord through the wondrous Holy Spirit. We need to be attentive to the rhythm of God's Spirit, realizing He will take us through all the seasons of our lives. Every day is a new day with the Lord in the garden of His grace.

In this book, I will focus on some of the main areas of spiritual growth. God uniquely designs your growth in the garden of grace. In your quiet time, He will teach you who He is, what He does, and what He says. He will map out your journey, guide your steps, and make you His woman in the world. You will learn who you are in Christ, what you have because of Christ, and how to grab His grace in the seasons of life, pray at the throne of grace, find a new day in your life through His promises, fall in love with Jesus, grace others in your life, dream His dreams, and find hope in your eternal future with Him. When you are a WIP, you learn to say, "By the grace of God, I'm not who I was, and by the grace of God, I'm not who I'm going to become."

So how can we grow spiritually? The Lord has led me to focus on five main areas over the years to grow deeper in my walk with Him: devotion, delight, discipleship, doctrine, and dedication. You will notice that these five areas encompass all the spiritual catalysts Willow Creek discovered in their study. When you focus on these five areas, you will grow deep in the garden of God's grace.

I focus on *devotion* to listen to the Lord and hear Him speak (Psalm 46:10). The more I grow in my quiet time, the more I grow in devotion.

I focus on *delight* to love the Lord with all my heart and soul and mind and strength (Matthew 22:37). As I worship the Lord, praise Him in church, partake in communion and baptism, and join together with others in the church community, I grow in delight.

I focus on *discipleship* to learn more about what it means to be a follower of Christ (2 Timothy 2:2). The more I connect with others who love the Lord, study the Bible with them, enjoy accountability, and then pass on what I've learned into the lives of others, the more I learn and grow in discipleship.

I focus on *doctrine* to live out what God works into my life (1 Timothy 4:6). The more I grow in my resolve and commitment to what I know is true in God's Word, the more I will grow in having sound doctrine (belief).

I focus on *dedication* to labor faithfully and well in service to the Lord (Romans 12:11 NIV). The more I grow in ministry and serving the Lord, the more I will grow in my dedication.

God assures us that He has begun a good work in us and will "perfect it until the day of Christ Jesus" (Philippians 1:6). Now *that's* growth in grace! God transforms us, and we respond to His gracious hand in our lives. We change and grow through His Spirit's work in us (2 Corinthians 3:18). The Holy Spirit is our spiritual growth trainer.

God changes us through the renewing of our minds (Romans 12:1-2). We grow as we walk by faith in God's Word, our spiritual growth manual (2 Corinthians 5:7). Always remember that spiritual growth takes time. Through the many seasons of life, God gives the grace of a new day, offers a plan for your life, and never leaves you. He is enough for whatever obstacles and difficulties you encounter as you walk with Him in the garden of grace.

✳

Many years ago I led a Bible study in San Diego. I used to meet weekly with a girl from that Bible study who became a dear friend. One week, at a morning breakfast meeting, I said, "You know what? I think you would be a great leader."

She responded, "Oh, I'm not mature enough for that. I could never do it. I don't know enough."

I left my thought with her, refusing to withdraw the idea. Every week from then on, I would say, "You are such a deep thinker. I think you would be an amazing discussion leader."

She would always respond, "I could never do that!"

After I moved away from San Diego, I had the opportunity to return and visit that Bible study. My friend led the discussion. I watched as she led the class through an in-depth examination of a very deep passage of Scripture. I felt as if I could have never led the discussion as masterfully as she did that day! I smiled, thinking back to those early days and thought, *Look how God has grown her up in her walk with Him.* Watching her teach brought such joy to my heart.

I wonder if the Lord experiences that same kind of joy, watching His work of grace in us unfold as we walk with Him in life. May we continue to grow in the garden of His grace, and may our lives offer up a fragrant aroma to the Lord and touch each person who crosses our paths.

Do you find yourself filled with a deeper desire to grow in your relationship with the Lord, to become more mature in your walk with Him? How do we actually live in this garden of grace so we can grow? How do we become mature so we can become the women God wants us to be—spiritual giants in God's kingdom? Let's continue on in the adventure of God's magnificent grace.

3

LIVING EXTRAVAGANTLY IN THE GARDEN

Brother Yun was born in 1958 in a small farming village, Liu Lao Zhuang, in the southern part of China's Henan province. When Yun was 16, his father became ill with cancer, and his mother was told, "There's no hope for your husband. Go home and prepare for his death." Yun watched his father suffer during this time. "Every night my dad lay in bed and could hardly breathe… My dad's sickness sapped all our money, possessions, and energy."

Yun's mother, who had heard about Jesus in earlier days, had grown weary, losing all hope. She was so distraught that she even contemplated suicide. But one night, she awakened and distinctly heard God speaking: *Jesus loves you.* The love of God was so real and present that she fell onto her knees and gave her life to the Lord. Calling a family meeting after her experience, she said, "Jesus is the only hope for Father." They all committed their lives to the Lord, laid their hands on Yun's father, and prayed, "Jesus, heal our father."

The next morning, miraculously, his father was better, and he recovered completely with no trace of the cancer that had ravaged his body. The family was so overwhelmed with excitement that they invited their family and friends to their home. Upon hearing the news, everyone knelt and gave their lives to Jesus. Yun said, "These were exciting times.

Not only did I receive Jesus as my personal Savior, but I also became a person who wanted to serve the Lord with all my heart."

Yun asked his mother, "Who is Jesus, really? What is He like?"

His mother replied, "Jesus is the Son of God, who died on the cross for us, taking all our sins and sicknesses. He recorded all His teachings in the Bible."

"Are there any words of Jesus left that I can read for myself?"

"No" said his mother, shaking her head. "All His words are gone. There is nothing left of His teaching."

What was Yun's response to such hopeless words? He said, "From that day on I earnestly wanted to have a copy of my own Bible. I asked my mother and fellow Christians what a Bible looked like, but no one knew." Bibles were rarely seen in the land at that time. But he was so hungry for a Bible of his own.

One day, a pastor answered the desire of his heart with these words, "The Bible is a heavenly book. If you want one, you'll need to pray to the God of heaven." Brother Yun took those words deep into his heart and prayed, *Lord, please give me a Bible. Amen.* For the next 100 days, he fasted and prayed, eating only a small bowl of rice each day. He thought he could not bear waiting much longer to hold God's Word in his hands.

Finally one day, Yun heard a knock at the door. He opened the door to discover two men, one with arm extended, holding out a red bag. Yun quickly looked inside. A Bible! Falling on his knees outside his home, he cried out, "Thank You, God. I will devour Your Word like a hungry child."

Few have ever feasted on the Word of God as Yun has. He refused to let his Bible out of his sight and used every available minute to read it. After reading through the Bible once, he memorized one chapter a day, finishing the entire book of Matthew in 28 days. He moved on to Acts, and after memorizing chapter 12, he sensed God calling him to ministry. *Yun, you shall go to the west and to the south to proclaim the gospel. You shall be My witness and testify on behalf of My name.*

Yun responded quickly. He packed his bags, grabbed his Bible, and walked toward the west. He met an old man named Yang who said, "I was on my way to see you. I was given the job to come and take you to the west, to Gao village." Evidently those in the village had heard the story of his Bible and wanted to meet the man who had received such a miraculous answer to prayer. When Yun arrived at the village, he met a hungry group of 40 men and women. He closed his eyes, held his Bible in the air, and said, "If you want to get a Bible, you must pray and seek God as I did." Then, burdened to teach the people but not knowing how to preach, he recited the entire book of Matthew. When he was finished, the entire village knelt before God with tears flowing down their cheeks. Yun spoke of the power of God's Word, saying, "That night, even though I was just sixteen years old, I learned that God's Word is powerful. When we share it with a burning heart, many people are touched. At that first meeting, thanks to the power of God, dozens of people had given their heart to Jesus."

That experience was only the beginning of Yun's adventure with his Lord. In his first year as a Christian, he led more than 2000 people to Jesus. In the following years, God used Brother Yun strategically as the catalyst for the house church movement in China. He and his coworkers conducted what they called "fleeing evangelism." They shared the gospel and then immediately left the area.

Brother Yun ministered in China for 23 years and was sent to prison three different times for a total of seven years in prison. He was tortured, mocked, and hung by handcuffs. He had no Bible in prison but meditated constantly on the Scriptures he had memorized. The Lord used the Word to encourage him and strengthen him in his faith.

After his second time in prison, Brother Yun established "oil stations" to teach the Bible to the thousands who were coming to the Lord. Those who came to the oil stations were required to read through the whole Bible and memorize the book of Matthew in the space of two months.

Brother Yun eventually escaped from China. But he looked at his years in prison as "prison seminary," where he learned many valuable lessons about the Lord that he could have never learned from a book. He speaks of the importance of possessing the sharp truth of the Word of God. "If you truly want to see God move, the two main things you must do is learn the Word of God and have obedience to do what God tells you to do."

Brother Yun is known by many as "the heavenly man." Authorities asked him one day, "What is your name, and where do you live?" Brother Yun replied, "I'm a heavenly man, and my home is in heaven." Those are words from someone who lives not in the world, but in the garden of grace. He said those words by faith because he knew from the Bible that life is in Christ, and his real home is with Him.

When you live in the garden of God's grace, you are a champion of faith, like Brother Yun. But faith does not blindly leap into an empty darkness. Your faith is objective, resting firmly on the truths in God's Word. You look at everything, even suffering, through the reality of God's Word. Paul outlines our way of life in the garden when he tells us that we live by faith (Romans 1:17) and walk by faith, not by sight (2 Corinthians 5:7).

Faith is your response to God's growth work in your heart. Spiritual growth does not occur by osmosis; it develops in your walk with God day by day and moment by moment. You don't just sit around, passive and uninvolved. God will ask for obedience, surrender, love, commitment, resolve, trust, patience, and more in your relationship with Him.

For example, God may ask you to forgive someone who has wronged you. Learning to forgive is a huge step in spiritual growth. You know you need to forgive, but quite honestly, you don't always feel it in your heart. Forgiving the offender is a huge challenge. But you can know that God empowers you for what He prompts in you. Your action of saying "I forgive you" requires faith. You take God at His Word, believing that He asks us to forgive and supplies the strength to forgive. And so you choose forgiveness instead of bitterness and resentment, extend your hand in love, and say, "I forgive you." That's walking by faith.

So your life in the garden where you will grow in grace is a life of faith. If you and I want to live, thrive, and grow in God's garden of grace, we will become experts in living and walking by faith. Brother Yun is an example of a champion of faith. He is serious about his faith. And we must learn from his example and wholeheartedly own the discipline of living by faith. Yun says, "If we belong to God, we must learn to put our own schedules away. We must bundle up all of our hopes, dreams, and future plans and lay them at the feet of Jesus. Even our very bodies, the Scriptures say, should be offered as living sacrifices. Such faith is holy and acceptable in God's sight."[1]

Walking by faith might be thought of as putting on "Bible glasses" so everything you see is filtered through the lens of God's Word. When you look at life, yourself, and others through the truths of God's Word, you live constantly with God's eternal perspective. The eternal perspective is the ability to see all of life from God's point of view and have what you see affect the way you live in the present.

In those early days in China, when his life was constantly in danger, Brother Yun always wore his Bible glasses. He rarely forgot to put them on because he had hidden God's Word in his heart, having memorized full chapters of the Bible. Why is Brother Yun such an example of faith, and why is he enjoying life in the garden of grace? He knows the Word of God. If you would like to grow in the garden of grace, you must learn to look at everything through the lens of the Bible. Then you will see clearly, walk in victory, and easily find the path to spiritual growth.

✳

He was a military man, a professional soldier in the Roman army. As a centurion, he commanded 100 men. And he loved his job. He had aspired to it, in fact. Stationed in Capernaum, he enjoyed the surrounding area with gentle rolling hillsides on the northwestern shore of the Sea of Galilee. But more than that, he loved the people who lived in Capernaum. He remembered the day when he gathered together a group of Jewish elders and said, "I'd like to build a synagogue for you here in Capernaum." And he had enjoyed his days—until now.

Recently, darkness had clouded his life, a storm beyond his own control. His favorite servant, who was dependable in every way and who seemed to anticipate his needs better than all his other men combined, was about to die. Devastated, the centurion spoke candidly to one of the Jewish elders who had become a good friend. "I cannot bear to lose my servant. My heart is broken. Surely there must be someone who can help us."

The Jewish elder was quiet for some time, and then he looked into the eyes of this Roman ruler, who had poured out kindness to all in their town. He said, "There is one possible answer—a man named Jesus, who many say is the Messiah. I have heard Him teach, and no one speaks the way He does. His words sound as though they are from God Himself."

"I am aware of this man teaching in Capernaum. My own men tell me that huge crowds have gathered to hear Him. But how can He help my servant, who is about to die?" asked the centurion.

"I've seen Jesus heal people. The blind see, and the paralyzed walk. I believe if He could just come to this house, He could heal your beloved servant."

The centurion shook his head. "I'm not worthy for such a man to come under my roof. I couldn't have Him come here. But yet, for the sake of my servant, I would do anything," he said with a hint of desperation in his voice. "Will you go to Jesus and implore Him to help us?"

"Yes, I'll go right away."

For the first time, the centurion felt relieved and at peace. Just to hear the name *Jesus* affected his sensibilities in a way he could not even define. He felt a care and concern from Jesus although he had not even met this man personally. He had only heard of Him, but just knowing about Jesus gave him assurance that whatever happened was God's answer for him. And God's answer, God's control and care would be enough for him whether his servant lived or died. The centurion looked out at the sky, thinking about this new place in his own life, a place of relief and rest in the arms of a God he was just beginning to know and understand.

A knock on the door broke through his deep thought. "Are you there? Open the door. We have news!"

Opening the door, he saw the excited faces of his friends. They were smiling—even exuberant. "Jesus is on His way. He's coming to heal your slave!"

"Coming here? To my house? No, I can't have Him under my roof. I'm not worthy. I want you to do something for me, if you are willing," said the centurion.

His friends weren't surprised at his reaction. They had hoped their excitement would convince him. Disappointed, they replied, "What do you want us to do for you? We'll do anything."

"Go to Jesus. Say these exact words: 'Lord, do not trouble Yourself further, for I am not worthy for You to come under my roof; for this reason I did not even consider myself worthy to come to You, but just say the word, and my servant will be healed. For I also am a man placed under authority, with soldiers under me; and I say to this one, "Go!" and he goes, and to another, "Come!" and he comes, and to my slave, "Do this!" and he does it'" (Luke 7:6-8).

The centurion watched his friends leave, determined in their mission on his behalf. Tears came to his eyes to think they would be willing to speak to Jesus for him. He stood outside, looked down the road, and wondered about Jesus.

In the meantime, his friends saw the crowd making their way with Jesus toward the centurion's home. They were swift in carrying out their assignment, yet afraid of offending Jesus, who clearly wanted to go to the centurion's house. Mustering up their courage, they told Jesus what the centurion had said, carefully using his exact words. But they were not prepared for His response.

Jesus could have possibly smiled and even laughed. With admiration for their friend, the centurion, Jesus turned to the crowd and said, "I say to you, not even in Israel have I found such great faith."

The centurion's friends had always known he was special. His kindness and humility were known to all Capernaum. But now, hearing Jesus marvel at their friend's faith, they were filled with awe.

Jesus turned to them and offered joyful words for their friend, the Roman centurion, "Go; it shall be done for you as you have believed" (Matthew 8:13).

Imagine the next moments. Perhaps the centurion stood outside for a long time just thinking about Jesus, wondering what He would say in response to his message. Not wanting to offend Him yet knowing his own unworthiness, he was certain of the power of Jesus' word, confident that it could overcome sickness.

"Sir, can I help you?"

Was he imagining that familiar request, having heard his servant say it a thousand times before?

"Sir, can I help you?"

The centurion turned. There was his beloved servant, smiling with a glint of mischief in his eyes. For he knew what it would mean to his master to have him back. And the moment he felt his sickness gone, replaced with a new strength, he wanted to surprise his master with the good news.

Holding wide his arms, with tears freely falling, the centurion embraced his beloved servant. For one brief moment, the master and slave expressed what they had always been—true friends. And now they were reunited by a touch from Jesus.

✳

Great faith. What is it, and how can we get it? The centurion had it, and Jesus applauded it. He marveled at it, in fact. So few understand and know great faith. When you look more closely at the story of the centurion, you see the secrets of great faith.

Great faith is wrapped up in understanding and applying the authority of God's Word. The centurion understood authority, for he had learned how to take orders from higher officials, and he was also an officer who only had to say the word, and his will was accomplished. Because he understood the authority of the word, he knew Jesus' word was enough to accomplish anything He commanded. The centurion exercised his faith when he said to Jesus, "Just say the word." He was telling Jesus, "It's enough that You have said it. I believe it. I know Your word is enough to accomplish whatever You say." And so faith is, as Ney Bailey defined it so well in her book *Faith Is Not a Feeling,* "taking God at His Word." And if faith is taking God at His Word, then faith requires knowledge of what God says. You cannot trust what you don't know. Faith appropriates God's words, enabling you to experience God's grace firsthand.

God's Word is absolutely essential to living by faith and growing spiritually. You need the Bible to grow deep in your faith. That statement might sound radical to some, but the Bible says, "Faith comes from hearing, and hearing by the word of Christ" (Romans 10:17). In fact, the Willow Creek study described this "breakthrough discovery": "The Bible is the most powerful catalyst for spiritual growth."[2] Indeed, there is no better way to spend time than to be alone with God in His Word. The apostle Paul encouraged an extravagant devotion to God's Word (Colossians 3:16). So let me ask you, how extravagant are you with God's Word these days?

I remember when I first surrendered my life to the Lord in college. I did not know or understand walking and living by faith. Faith was a complete mystery to me. The Bible was almost a closed book for me because I had only barely begun reading it. When I first heard Ney Bailey define faith as taking God at His Word, I reasoned that if faith pleased God, then more than anything else, I needed to know what He said in His Word. I launched out on a course of life in God's Word that continues to this day.

How can we move from a life of frustration and distance from God to a vibrant, dynamic, growing relationship with God? Realize that God is extending His hand to you, inviting you to walk with Him and grow with Him in the garden of grace. Very simply, grab His hand and launch out on the journey of spiritual growth.

You will need a spiritual growth plan to guide you. People say that if you fail to plan, you plan to fail. Every year I ask God to design my spiritual growth plan. I pray, think, and plan so I can continue to grow in my walk of faith in the garden of grace. I like to ask five main questions that address the five essential areas of spiritual growth.

1. DEVOTION: *Lord, how will we spend quiet time together this year?*

I anticipate the new year and my favorite time each day with the Lord—my quiet time. When I sit with Him in the morning with my Bible open, pencil in hand, and *Quiet Time Notebook* at my side, I know God is going to speak. In my spiritual growth planning for the year, I look at all my available Bible reading plans (including devotional Bibles, Bible studies, chapter reading, and reading guides, like the online "Encounter with God" from Scripture Union) and ask God to help me know where He would like me to focus. Then I look through my growing stack of books I want to read and choose three or four to use in my quiet time. Devotionals like *Daily Light* and *My Utmost for His Highest* are standards I use periodically in my devotions. I leaf through my *Quiet Time Notebook,* pulling out used pages and adding new journal, prayer, and study pages. Then I put everything in my quiet time basket, and I'm ready to grow in the new year.[3]

2. DELIGHT: *Lord, how can I love and glorify You this year?*

I review my worship times and my involvement in church. If you aren't involved in a church that teaches God's Word and provides good fellowship, great worship, and opportunities to serve the Lord, ask God to help you find one. I am careful about spending time with others who love God and will encourage me in my walk with Him. Most of the time, you will find these good friends in your church. Fellowship helps you grow, for you need encouragement from fellow grace walkers (1 Thessalonians 5:11; Hebrews 3:13; 10:24-25). Spiritual growth is not a strictly personal undertaking; it also occurs in the context of community (Ephesians 2:19-22). You are part of the church, the people of God, and a fellow citizen with the saints. Find good friends who love the Lord, think deeply, and will take time to share their love for God and His Word. Always look for others who will ask, "What is God teaching you?"

3. DISCIPLESHIP: *Lord, whom will I learn with, and who will learn with me this year?*

I always join a Bible study with others who also love the Lord. I love the accountability a group Bible study offers. You can join a study at your church, with your friends, and even online.[4] I plan out my year and decide what I'll study, how I'll study, and with whom I'll study the Bible. I also look online for video curriculum and study books I can use on my own to go deeper in my learning and growth with the Lord.[5]

4. DOCTRINE: *Lord, what main theme in Your Word do You want me to focus on this year?*

When I teach theology at Biola University, I always begin the class by saying, "All of you are theologians. My goal is for you to be *good* theologians." We all believe something. I want us to believe the truth in God's Word. Your beliefs determine how you live. Every year I ask the Lord to show me an area of focus so I can learn and grow. Over the years, I've chosen to study the character of God, the promises of God, books of the Bible, and more. Each year I ask the Lord to give me a verse for the year and word for the year. These words have included *trust, hope, faith, believe,* and *wait.* As God shows me what is true, I write out what I believe in my journal. Then I apply the truth from the Bible to my life by writing affirmations and commitments to the Lord.

For example, I learn in Romans 15:4 that the Scriptures bring encouragement. I might write, *Lord, thank You for the gracious gift of Your*

Word and its encouragement in my life. Help me run to Your Word for encouragement and hope in difficult times. God will always lead you to new affirmations of grace as you walk with Him in the garden (see the appendix for more affirmations of grace). I have noticed that the Holy Spirit, who uses God's Word in my life, brings me to decisions of commitment and surrender to the Lord. I have learned more and more to pay attention to those decisions and yield instead of wrestle.[6]

5. DEDICATION: *Lord, how will I serve You this year?*

When the Holy Spirit works in you, He leads you into ministry. He may prompt you to serve Him in a myriad of ways—in your church, in your neighborhood, and even on the Internet. As you step out in faith and serve the Lord, you will grow deeper in your relationship with Him.

I like to think through my goals and consider ways I can serve the Lord in the upcoming year. I may include something new, like writing a blog. Or I may write a new quiet time book and teach the study at my church.

✳

You may be thinking, *Catherine, you're really serious about the Bible, quiet time, and spiritual growth, aren't you?* Yes, I am, because I believe God is serious about our spiritual growth. He wants us to be mature believers who feed on solid food, not milk-fed and immature Christians (Hebrews 5:11-14). You see the sincerity of God's purpose for you in these words from Paul: "He who began a good work in you will perfect it until the day of Christ Jesus" (Philippians 1:6). He wants you to draw near to Him so that He may draw near to you (James 4:8). He has given you everything you need to grow close to Him, which is the ultimate goal in your spiritual growth. He's given you His Word to speak to you, teach you, and change you, and He's given you the indwelling Holy Spirit to apply His Word to your life.

Our current culture has lost the vision in many ways for this one-on-one, personal relationship with God. Award-winning author and columnist Cathleen Falsani says that many of us are "gasping for air and grasping for God, but fleeing from a kind of religious experience that has little to do with anything sacred or gracious."[7] We are obsessed with church organization, programs, and new plans. In fact, many are turning to ideas and plans promoted by the largest, most publicized churches. And while many of these ideas have value in promoting church growth, we cannot forget the main focus of drawing near to God and knowing Him. Without our personal relationship with God, all the best ideas become merely religion. Jesus spoke most strongly against the Pharisees, who were very religious but missed the relationship and chose law instead of grace.

When you give time and attention to the five essential areas of spiritual growth, your relationship with God and your faith will grow and grow and grow. You will discover that the Word of God shapes everything you do to grow spiritually.

Always remember you are a work in progress—a WIP. Willow Creek discovered through their study that spiritual growth is an intricate, multidimensional process. Greg Hawkins and Cally Parkinson write in their book *Follow Me,* "Spiritual growth is a highly individual process, full of mysterious moments that crystallize and catalyze our faith."[8] They liken the spiritual catalysts of spiritual beliefs and attitudes, church activities, spiritual disciplines, and spiritual community to musical instruments performing in an orchestra. They work together to develop spiritual growth leading to maturity.

If you have access to a Bible, then thank God you have more opportunity to grow than do many people in parts of the world where owning a Bible is against the law. And you can know that down through history, numerous men and women gave their lives so you could hold a Bible in your hands and grow in your faith.

Why is faith so important to your life in the garden of grace? Because eternal truths are not always seen, yet they are absolutely real and true (see 2 Corinthians 4:18). Sometimes your circumstances will seem to oppose the truth of the promises from God in His Word. And your enemy, the devil, also known as the father of lies, will try to trip you up. He whispers everything that is untrue and contrary to God's Word, prompting fear and worry in the soul (John 8:44). What and whom will you believe—God or your circumstance? His Word or your feelings of fear and anxiety? Truth or the father of lies? Therein lies the incredible value of an exercised, disciplined life of faith in the garden of grace. Don't believe the lie. Instead, believe, receive, and live God's grace.

I received an e-mail from a friend whose wife was laid off from a job she loved. He asked for prayer for his wife, who was "taking it hard." Then he wrote these words: "God has us right where He wants us (and where we need to be)...totally stretched out on Him in faith! As Brennan Manning puts it, 'ruthless trust.'" I ached for my friends, but I loved the husband's words. How could he express such hope in such a difficult situation? The only answer is that he knows what God says and believes God's words. It's one thing to believe *in* God but quite another to *believe God*. A big faith believes God.

My faith is challenged when I am surprised by a trial that calls into question everything I know to be true from God's Word. When our economic situation required me to find a new full-time job many years ago, I thought, *No problem. I've got degrees, experience, and the Lord. He'll find me a job.* But I couldn't find one. God promised to supply my needs (Philippians 4:19). In fact, I knew His name was *Yahweh Jireh,* the God who provides (Genesis 22:14). He promised a plan for my life and a future and a hope (Jeremiah 29:11).

So where was my job? Was God's Word true or not? In my trial of faith, I had to decide whom and what I would believe—God and His Word, or my feelings and sight. Thankfully, the indwelling Holy Spirit helped me hold on to God's Word, believe Him, and pray for a job in His time and in His way. God added promises to my arsenal of faith. I found strength in the promise that my times were in His hand (Psalm 31:15). I rested in the promise that God would indeed accomplish what concerned me (Psalm 138:8). And finally, God taught me to wait in faith, patient for His perfect timing in my life to provide everything I need (Psalm 130:5-6). Not only that, I learned a new name of God—*El Shaddai* (Genesis 17:1). Drawing near to *El Shaddai,* I learned that He is all-sufficient, enough for every life experience. Some aspects of spiritual growth are possible only in difficult times like mine. In the crucible of our faith, we are led deeper into our knowledge of God, and eventually we experience Him in new ways that we would never have known without the fiery trial.

Oswald Chambers writes in *My Utmost for His Highest* about faith's value:

> At the bar of common sense Jesus Christ's statements may seem mad; but bring them to the bar of faith, and you begin to find with awestruck spirit that they are the words of God. Trust entirely in God and when He brings you to the venture, see that you take it. We act like pagans in a crisis, only one out of a crowd is daring enough to bank his faith in the character of God.[9]

I dared to believe God during my own trial of faith, and I eventually experienced God's amazing provision of a job.

You will discover your faith tested at times by various trials (James 1:2-4). When your faith rests on God's Word, you will experience a new and stronger faith on the other side of the trial. Nineteenth-century writer J.B. Stoney explains how trials grow our faith: "Real faith is always increased by opposition, while false confidence is damaged and discouraged by it."[10] When your faith is proven to be genuine because it is resting on the unchangeable, immovable facts in God's Word, great praise and glory and honor will result (1 Peter 1:7). And you will rejoice in the day when Christ Himself rewards your faith.

Have you learned the secret of walking by faith? Is your faith being tested in your current circumstance? Dear friend, I encourage you to put on your Bible glasses, draw near to your Lord, review your affirmations of grace, and learn how to live by faith in this garden of grace. And who knows, perhaps the Lord will commend your faith as He did the centurion's, and perhaps you will be like Brother Yun, influencing thousands in their faith. You can count on this one truth, promised in God's Word: When you live by faith, you will experience spiritual growth and Christ at work in and through you.

> GOD, teach me lessons for living
>   so I can stay the course.
> Give me insight so I can do what you tell me—
>   my whole life one long, obedient response.
> Guide me down the road of your commandments;
>   I love traveling this freeway!
> Give me a bent for your words of wisdom,
>   and not for piling up loot.
> Divert my eyes from toys and trinkets,
>   invigorate me on the pilgrim way.
> Affirm your promises to me—
>   promises made to all who fear you.
> Deflect the harsh words of my critics—
>   but what you say is always so good.
> See how hungry I am for your counsel;
>   preserve my life through your righteous ways!
>   (Psalm 119:33-40 MSG).

Part 2

The Gift of Grace

CATERPILLARS CAN FLY

Amy Carmichael had a propensity for doing just what she was told not to do. She and her brothers had been told that the seeds of the nearby laburnum tree were poisonous.

"I wonder how many we can eat before we die!" Amy said to her two brothers. They felt uncomfortable after eating their share and were all sent to their rooms to think about what they'd done wrong. Amy seemed to enjoy rebellion and often tested her parents' boundaries. When she was told how bad she was, she used to think, *If only you knew how much naughtier I could be, you wouldn't think I'm naughty at all.*[1]

She grew up in an atmosphere of Bible reading, prayer, and attending church. When Amy was three years old, she determined to test what she had learned from her mother about prayer. Kneeling beside her bed, she fervently prayed, *Lord, give me blue eyes.* She was confident such an answer to prayer would be no problem for God. She jumped out of bed the next morning and ran to the mirror. She was shocked. "Brown eyes, they're still brown." She learned, "'No' is also an answer." She also learned that prayer is not like a magic formula.

At 12, Amy attended boarding school in Yorkshire. The restrictions and taboos of the school challenged Amy's free spirit. One night in particular, she determined to break the rules and led all the schoolgirls to the roof to view a spectacular comet display. When they walked through the door and out on the roof, they were face-to-face with the principal and teachers. Amy's heart sank. *I'll be expelled. I know it.* They knew she was the ringleader, but in the end, they forgave her.

God had His hand on Amy and knew she would be His. He intended to give this girl with the propensity to rebel against rules the ability to love and serve Him. One day she would no longer crawl on the ground, tied to her sin, but instead would be given wings to soar with Him.

Near the end of her three years in boarding school, Amy attended a series of Children's Mission Board meetings highlighting speaker Edwin Arrowsmith. The worship leader chose the simple children's hymn by Anna B. Warner, "Jesus Loves Me." Amy sang the words along with everyone else. Quietly, before the Lord, she realized she needed to open the door of her life to Him. And in those moments, Amy Carmichael opened her heart to Jesus.

That day, at 15, Amy began a new journey with the Lord. God began working in her, making her into His magnificent masterpiece and leading her into His plans and purposes in the world. Ultimately, God called Amy to travel to India and spend 53 years there without furlough in Tamil Nadu, South India. She founded Dohnavur Fellowship, a sanctuary for more than a thousand children, many of whom were rescued out of temple prostitution. She was *Amma* (mother) to her children. Once she found her place of service in India, she realized why God gave her brown eyes. Her God-given eye color enabled her to more easily blend in with the Indian culture.

Amy's adventure with the Lord created a ripple effect, influencing people's lives long after her own 83 years. One person Amy influenced was an Indian girl named Mimosa. Amy recalled the first time she saw Mimosa: "She was standing out in the sunshine...a radiant thing in a crimson and orange *sari*...like a bird from the woods in her colours and her jewels, but her eyes were large and soft and gentle, more like a fawn's than a bird's."[2] She had accompanied her father to visit her sister, Star, who lived with Amy and others at Dohnavur Fellowship.

In those short moments, Amy told Mimosa about a loving God and His Son, Jesus Christ. Then Amy tried to convince the Hindu father to leave Mimosa along with Star.

"No," he replied. "She cannot stay. One shame is enough."

Mimosa begged, "Oh, Father, Father!"

But he would not allow her to stay. Amy's last memory of Mimosa for 22 years was of those big brown eyes trying to smile through her tears.

Mimosa's family could tell something had happened to her. How could that short time with Amy have made such a difference? But Mimosa had drunk in Amy's words. And she had known in those moments that God, the Creator, was the living Father who loved her. She had sensed the "great love," as she called it, of Jesus Christ. By the time she had left, she was confident His eternal love surrounded her.

When she arrived home, things looked and felt brand-new. Had her surroundings changed? No, but Mimosa had changed. She knew she could no longer worship the Hindu gods and rub ashes on her forehead in allegiance to Siva, one of the gods. Her family was perplexed and then enraged. She was often beaten. Gradually, she learned patience as she endured the mistreatment. Amy described Mimosa's experience in those early days:

> Was the child forgotten by the Love that had shone upon her? Love never forgets. Gradually through her troubles a gentle sense of still being loved stole in upon her soul. She knew, though how she could never have told, that the God she would not forsake had not forsaken her. And all alone, without a single friend who understood, or a single touch of human compassion, she was comforted.[3]

According to the caste custom, Mimosa was later secluded in a small area of the house, never allowed to leave until she married. But God was watching over her, and His love continued to surround her, offering hope and encouragement in the smallest overtures. At 17, Mimosa was given in marriage to a man who lost his land and had no way to make a living. What's worse, he refused to work. Mimosa stepped out of the cultural norms for Indian women and worked in the fields to earn a living. She took her firstborn son with her as she worked.

Eventually, she felt the weight of the great burden of her miseries. She put her little baby in a crude hammock and watched as he fell asleep. Then she walked to a quiet place, alone with the Lord, and sobbed. Crying aloud, she prayed, *O God, my husband has deceived me, his brother has deceived me, even my mother has deceived me, but You will not deceive me...I am not offended with You. Whatever You do is good. What should I do without You? You are the Giver of health and strength and will to work. Are not these things better than riches or people's help?* She then knelt in the open field and spread the bottom of her *sari* out before the Lord, holding it open, as though waiting to receive provision from Him. She then prayed, *I am an emptiness for You to fill.* How did she know to pray such a prayer? Only through God. She left refreshed and invigorated, confident He had heard and answered.

Mimosa was alone in the world among her people, a lover of God, a worshipper in a place dedicated to many gods. But she never traveled alone, for Jesus was with her. She suffered while caring for her sons and husband, working long hours and often going without food so they could eat. As her sons grew, Mimosa longed to move them to a safe environment where they could grow as Christians.

One day she received a letter from her sister, Star, who was still living at Dohnavur. Mimosa responded, asking through a dictated letter if she could bring two of her boys to live at Dohnavur. "When might I come?" she asked, having received her husband's initial consent. Later, Mimosa's husband buckled under the coercion of the Hindu caste system and refused to let her go. But one day, Mimosa grabbed her children and delivered all but her baby to Dohnavur Fellowship. She returned to her husband for a short time, but he despised and ignored her. Finally, she decided to go back to Dohnavur, learn to read, and grow in her knowledge of God from the Bible.

After Mimosa learned and grew in her relationship with Christ, she went back to her husband, intent on winning him to Christ. During the next 30 years, Mimosa saw her husband turn to the Lord. She continued visiting Dohnavur frequently, meeting with and ministering to others who wanted to see the woman who held fast to Christ for more than 20 years with no human encouragement or help.

Mimosa is just one of thousands whose lives were changed because of Amy Carmichael's commitment to Christ. Amy was willing to sacrifice a comfortable existence in Ireland to serve in a remote area in India. She trusted God even when she was injured and spent most of the last 20 years of her life in bed. Even then, God enabled her to write books, many still in print today.

How could Amy Carmichael live such a dedicated, sacrificial life for the Lord? One day Amy received a letter from a young woman who was considering life as a missionary. She asked, "What is missionary life like?"

Amy's response was simple, "Missionary life is a chance to die." Her answer revealed a heart surrendered to Jesus. Amy's life in India was filled with many hardships. But Amy was a brand-new person, changed by God. He had given her wings, enabling her to fly in the face of even the greatest impossibilities there in a Hindu culture desperately needing God.

And the story of change goes on and on. Prostitutes who come to Jesus are given new life. Robbers who know Jesus stop stealing from people. And persecutors of Christians, like the apostle Paul, become missionaries for the gospel of Christ. When people come to know Jesus, they are no longer who they were, but experience a brand-new life.

✳

Can people really change? Years ago, a barber's union in Chicago advertised that a certain brand of soap would change one's life. Union officials went down to Madison Street and picked up the filthiest derelict they could find and used their soap on him, giving a bath, a shave, shampoo...the works. They bought the poor man a fine suit, put him up in a beautiful hotel suite, and advertised in the newspapers the next day: "See what we have done, we have made a new man with soap."

Of course it didn't really work, for he was no new man at all. Some weeks later a small item on page 13 of the paper stated, "The man made over by the barbers' union was found last night on Madison Street, drunk, dirty, and disillusioned."

If we could change ourselves, why are more and more people every year hovering between the pain of living and the pain of dying? In 1992, more teenagers and young adults died from suicide than died from cancer, heart disease, AIDS, birth defects, stroke, pneumonia, influenza, and chronic lung disease combined. A book on how to take one's life has made it to the bestseller lists.

A picture of two beautiful teenage girls caught my eye in the *Los Angeles Times*. I was horrified to read the article describing how they had carried out a suicide pact. Their note read, "Don't forget us, we won't forget you, we just couldn't handle life anymore." People are literally dying for a change. I receive countless letters from drug addicts in prison who are desperate to change and receive brand-new lives. Many in the world today may wonder, *Is there any hope for a person who longs for change? Can the old be made new?*

✳

The story of her life could have been titled *The Moment That Cost Her Everything*. She knew she was entering a dark road by saying yes to the unlawful embrace for a breath of excitement or just a drop of kindness. Who really knew the reasons for her choice? She was not even certain what drove her into the arms of another man. But now she was caught. She could not run away. And worse, the scribes and Pharisees were taking her to Jesus, a prophet. What she did not know was that the Pharisees were using her for their own plan to find a way to seize and arrest Jesus.

She looked up at the gleaming stone pillars of the temple. In another time, before this defining moment, she might have derived a certain spiritual calmness from the religious surroundings. But all the bustling activity faded into the background of her personal life-and-death drama. She knew she would likely die. She could not even bear to think about what came next. Terrified, she looked ahead to the temple court, wondering where she was being taken.

Straight ahead, she saw a large crowd. As they neared the crowd, she sensed a strange sort of peace, something unlike anything she had felt before. She strained to see whom everyone was looking at, and she noticed a particular man in the distance. He must be a rabbi, teaching those in attendance.

As the scribes and Pharisees pushed her nearer the crowd, the man stopped talking and looked at her. She would never forget His look. That face, those eyes... The kindness and love pulled her into His gaze and fixed her focus on Him.

The crowd, almost in slow motion, stepped back. She felt herself dragged and then almost thrown into the center of the court. Her accusers stood at a distance, leaving her separate and alone, face-to-face with the rabbi.

"Teacher, this woman has been caught in adultery, in the very act. Now in the Law Moses commanded us to stone such women; what then do you say?" (John 8:4-5).

Now her heart was pounding with fear, her eyes downcast with embarrassment, her face red with humiliation. Helpless, defenseless, she looked up into the rabbi's face. But He was not looking at her. He wasn't looking at her accusers. His eyes were on the ground. He refused to join in the crowd's contempt. He would not enter into their derision and scorn.

Tears rolled down her face onto the dirt. She was shocked at His reaction to their words. She had never experienced such an overwhelming gift from a man. Jesus was giving her something she had never received—especially from these religious men. Acceptance, respect, kindness...and not because she earned any of His gracious regard for her. He simply embodied grace and poured it out in large measure on her, an undeserving sinner. She could tell He knew her through and through. But this astounding grace was real. His treatment of her was an inexpressibly gracious gift, a stark contrast from the disdain of her accusers, who were more concerned about her wrongdoing than her life.

What was Jesus doing now? Kneeling down, He was writing something with His finger in the sand of the temple floor. Could it be names? Was it the sins of those in the crowd?

Again, her accusers pressed a response from the teacher. He stood straight up, and when He did, she thought He appeared ten feet tall. He said only a few words. She was not even sure what He meant.

"He who is without sin among you, let him be the first to throw a stone at her." Then He knelt down and wrote again in the dirt.

In confusion and terror, she fixed her pleading eyes on this man who had uttered the strange death sentence. She braced herself for the impact of the first stone...and waited.

A heavy stillness enveloped the crowd, and in the sudden quiet, Jesus' words echoed in each accuser's conscience.

Only Jesus understood the hearts in attendance at the meeting in the temple courts that day. He knew there was no difference between a woman caught in adultery or a religious leader claiming to be righteous. Both were unable to keep all the law. Both adulterer and Pharisee broke at least one command of the law. And to stumble in one point of the law was to become guilty of all of it (James 2:10). Both were in need of a Savior, but neither yet understood.

The older ones in the crowd left first, one by one. Why? Because they had lived long enough to know that they weren't perfect and that they could not change themselves. The younger ones took a little longer, but in the end only an adulterous woman stood before the King of kings and Lord of lords, Jesus Christ.

He stood and addressed her directly, "Woman, where are they? Did no one condemn you?"

Shocked, she replied, her eyes gradually opening to the identity of this one standing before her. "No one, Lord." No longer enslaved to a life of sin, she served a new Master.

Jesus then said the happiest words any sinner can hear. "I do not condemn you, either. Go. From now on sin no more."

No stone was thrown that day. Instead, grace was extravagantly lavished on a sinful woman set free and sent out with new life.

✳

Have you ever felt like that woman—caught, guilty, and convicted of your sin? Without a hope in the world? When you are born again, becoming a Christian through receiving Christ into your heart, God's grace makes you a brand-new person. This is no mere alteration, but a metamorphosis. In Christ you are a new creature; the old things have passed away, and new things have come (2 Corinthians 5:17). The old life and new life are radically different, as Jesus revealed when He warned against putting new wine in old wineskins. He explained that new wine goes into fresh wineskins, and both are preserved (Matthew 9:17). He does not work with old, flawed materials, but instead gives brand-new life—and not just any life. The new life is His life in you.

We see a beautiful example of metamorphosis when a lowly caterpillar becomes a beautiful butterfly. Have you ever considered the life cycle of a butterfly? It begins with an egg, and from that egg comes a little furry and sometimes ugly caterpillar. The caterpillar eventually produces enough silk to create a cocoon. In that cocoon, the caterpillar is liquefied, and something new is formed: a butterfly with wings and the ability to fly. This new creature struggles to break free of the cocoon. The struggle is necessary to develop the strength to be able to fly. Once free of the cocoon, the butterfly extends its wings, blood travels to every area of the wings, and the butterfly begins to fly.

Through your transformation when you are born again, you become a believer who is indwelt by the Holy Spirit. A metamorphosis occurs, and you are given new life. You have a brand-new identity in Christ. Grace makes you who you are. You no longer are a caterpillar living in the dirt of this world, but a butterfly that is set free to fly. Those letters BC and AD apply to your own life in a new way.

Before Christ, we knew only a life of sin resulting in the penalty of death (Romans 3:23; 6:23). But through our union with Christ, we are identified with His death on the cross. We experience death to the old life (Romans 7:4-6). Our death with Christ leads to resurrection life—real life—as we are transformed into the image of Christ. Through your amazing metamorphosis into a new creation in Christ, you are set free to love and serve Christ forever (Romans 8). And you are free to grow.

Why are these truths so important? Because you need to know that once you have entered into a relationship with Christ, you are no longer who you were. Christ lives in you through the indwelling Holy Spirit. And He is at work in you, transforming your heart, character, and life so they reflect His new life in you. He does in you what you could never do for yourself. You become the person God wants you to be. He changes you, growing you from the inside out. A new person (Jesus) and power (the Holy Spirit) live in you, and you can live supernaturally, doing what you could never do before and becoming who you could never be in your own strength. He sets you free to say no to sin and yes to Him.

Because of your new life in Christ, you are able to say yes to God's desires for you—yes to walking in a manner worthy of the Lord (Colossians 1:10), yes to thinking on what is true (Philippians 4:8-9), yes to seeking first God's kingdom and righteousness (Matthew 6:33), yes to holiness (1 Peter 1:13-16), yes to following Christ (Philippians 3:12-14), yes to running your race and fixing your eyes on Jesus (Hebrews 12:1-2), yes to carefully walking in wisdom (Ephesians 5:15), yes to abstaining from every form of evil (1 Thessalonians 5:15), and yes to making the best use of your time (Colossians 4:5-6). Not only *can* you say yes, you will *want* to say yes to God. Your freedom in grace doesn't mean license to sin, but living to God in righteousness and godliness (Titus 2:11-14).

Why live in the filth and dirt of the evil, godless world when you can live in the sparkling, beautiful palace of holiness and God's glory? Dallas Willard comments that sinful things just won't consume your mind and heart as they once did: "As formation in Christlikeness progresses, they simply won't matter. In fact, they will seem ridiculous and uninteresting."[4]

Does this metamorphosis mean you will never sin again? John says we will sin. While on earth, we are still in our fleshly bodies, and we face the foes of the world and the devil (1 John 1:8-10). However, when we sin, we are to confess our sin and live in the light of God's forgiveness. And remember, all your sins are forgiven (Colossians 1:14). The prison doors are open, the penalty is paid, the debt is cancelled, and you are set free to joyfully walk and grow with your Lord in the garden of grace.

What about negative feelings? What if I don't feel forgiven? What if I do not yet feel like the butterfly? We've got to remember we are not condemned (Romans 8:1). Joseph Cooke explains what this means:

> Jesus' death provides for forgiveness and healing of the disorders in my spirit that give birth to negative feelings. I don't have to hide them. I don't have to doll them up. They're just part of what I am, and God loves me as I am even though, as I say, He is at work to heal me, to change me into the image of the Lord (2 Corinthians 3:18).[5]

Dallas Willard points out the place of feelings in our lives:

> Feelings have a crucial role in life, but they must not be taken as a *basis* for action or character change. That role falls to insight, understanding, and convictions of truth,

which will always be appropriately accompanied by feeling. Feelings are not fundamental in the nature of things, but become so if we assign them that role in life, and then life will not go on as it should. Many sincere, professing Christians suffer in their walk with God because they made a commitment prompted by a feeling of "need" and not by insight into how things are with God and their soul.[6]

More and more, you will grow in appropriating the power of God, saying no to the old things and yes to the new (Ephesians 4:22-24). Moment by moment, you will grow in your ability to live and walk by faith as you say yes to God and no to sin. You are forgiven and set free to love and serve and live with Him forever. God is the one who causes the growth, the transformation (1 Corinthians 3:7). These are wonderful gifts from the God of all grace. Affirm His grace in your life. Believe it, receive it, and live it. And as you are transformed, you will learn to fly, to soar on the heights with God, doing what you were meant to do. Christ lives His life in and through you to touch a lost, hurting world.

✳

Kayla was so excited to get her first bicycle. She had seen her dad riding, and she wanted a bicycle more than anything. But she soon discovered riding it was a lot more difficult than she imagined. While she was asleep one night, her father attached something to the bicycle to make riding it a whole lot easier for his beloved daughter. He put training wheels on the back wheel to help steady the bike so Kayla could ride. She jumped on the bike and was already halfway down the sidewalk in front of their house. "Dad, look! I can ride!"

Before long, our Kayla was ready to join the big guys with a real bike and no training wheels. She was more grown-up and ready to ride in a whole new way. One morning she came down the stairs to find a brand-new shiny bicycle. It was bigger than her first bike and had no training wheels. She wheeled it outside, and away she rode.

What made the difference between riding the first bike with training wheels and the bigger bicycle without them? She was more mature, more grown-up. She had changed and learned how to ride a bicycle. Now she could handle the bigger bike and ride without training wheels. Someday, her bicycle is going to seem like child's play, for she will be eyeing her driver's license and getting behind the wheel of a car.

When I first became a Christian, I had no idea how to grow spiritually. But I knew I was not the same person. Something had happened inside me. I felt as if I had been set free. My feelings of inferiority lessened with each new truth about Christ's acceptance of me and His work in me. I became less concerned with others' opinions and much more occupied with what God said in His Word. I found a love for others that was unexplainable. I actually desired to show kindness, even toward unkind people. My transformation is an ongoing process (Philippians 1:6; 2:13). I am not who I was, and I am not who I am becoming in the strength of Christ and the power of the Holy Spirit. When we grow in grace, we become more and more who we are in Christ.

Recently, I walked into our Quiet Time Ministries office and saw Sandy, one of our volunteers, busily at work inputting names and addresses into our database. I told her I was thinking about and studying spiritual transformation.

She smiled knowingly and said, "You know, this last year I've gone through some fiery trials. And you know what God is teaching me? Three words: *He is here.* I am learning that He is present in my life. Those truths are taking me deeper in my intimacy with Christ and transforming me into a woman who trusts Him with my very life."

I nodded. "Sandy, I'm learning to trust Him more also. I find that He is building me into a stronger, more trusting person. And yet, in myself, I feel weaker. It must be His strength, courage, and boldness in me."

We need to understand that sanctification—our new set-apart life—is a one-time occurrence with ongoing, transformational, life-altering results. We have been sanctified, but we are also being sanctified (Hebrews 10:14). He is at work in us, conforming us to the image of Christ, who lives in us (Romans 8:29). Our Lord has laid out a path for our spiritual growth so that we will continue becoming who we already are—masterpieces of grace for His glory (Ephesians 2:10).

✳

Deion Sanders grew up in Fort Myers, Florida. He started playing football at the age of eight and was a star from the very beginning. Every time he touched the ball, he scored a touchdown. Baseball was the same—he was always the best on his team. His senior year in high school, he was offered a contract to play baseball for the Kansas City Royals. Instead, he went to college at Florida State University, where he lettered in football, baseball, and track. He actually played professional baseball for the Yankees while attending college. In 1989 he was drafted by the Atlanta Falcons in the first round. In 1995 Deion was signed as a free agent by the Dallas Cowboys. Deion Sanders is the only athlete to have played in both a World Series and a Super Bowl, playing both professional baseball and football at the same time.

Recognized as the league's most dominant coverage cornerback at one time, Sanders was capable of single-handedly taking half of the field away from opposing offenses, and teams often simply refused to throw the football his way. His elite reputation as a performer was backed up by his production. He was selected to seven Pro Bowls while collecting 41 career interceptions and 20 regular-season touchdowns.

Someone who achieved so much should have been on top of the world, but Deion Sanders wasn't. He had everything—money, possessions, power—everything that the world holds in such high esteem. But in 1996 he was experiencing inner turmoil.

There I was, driving 70 miles an hour down the highway, just looking for a place to end it all...How had I come to such a low point in my life? Deion Sanders! Prime Time! Mr. Millionaire Athlete and all that...What had happened to me?...

None of my success on the field could prepare me for the crisis in my life that led to my suicide attempt. When I took that deadly plunge, I had reached the end of my rope. I was struggling with just about everything in my life. God stripped me of all of the comforts, all the success, and all the relationships that I had depended on. He was bringing me to the point where I could see His hand in my life... Miraculously, I walked away without a scratch...

Late one night, I opened the Bible to a passage that said, "If you confess with your mouth the Lord Jesus and believe in your heart that God has raised Him from the dead, you will be saved. For with the heart one believes unto righteousness, and with the mouth confession is made unto salvation" (Romans 10:9-10). The words hit me like a ton of bricks. I knew they were meant for me. At that moment I put my trust in Jesus and asked Him into my life. When I found Christ, I found what I had been missing all those years. Only then was I able to trust in God's will for my life. I have a new sense of peace about what happens on and off the field. I have a passionate hunger for the things of God, and each day I'm feeding on His Word. Success almost ruined my life, but thank God, I came to Him just in the nick of time. And that has made all the difference.[7]

Caterpillars do indeed become butterflies with wings to fly. God radically changed Deion Sanders' heart. And those around him knew for a fact that he was not the same man he was before.

Omar Stoutmire, a safety who was drafted by the Cowboys, had gotten involved in the party scene and lost his direction in life. When he joined the Cowboys, he was looking to put his life back in order. Then he met Deion Sanders, and the two became great friends. One day, Omar decided to go all the way and give his life to Christ.

The changed life of Deion Sanders has impacted those around him both on and off the field. How could a man who tried to end his life become someone who walks every day with meaning and purpose? Only one way—through Jesus Christ. In an interview with *EP News,* Sanders said, "I've buried the old Deion Sanders; there is a new one walking strong and healthy because of what the Lord has done in my life."

Do you feel like Deion Sanders did? Are you like a caterpillar that longs for a metamorphosis into a beautiful butterfly? Would you like to be transformed from the inside out? Receive the gift of salvation and forgiveness of sins by grace through faith (Ephesians 2:8-9). You may give your life to Jesus by praying a simple prayer like this:

> *Lord Jesus, I need You. Thank You for dying on the cross for my sins. I invite You to come into my life, forgive my sins, and make me the woman You want me to be. I come to You in Jesus' name. Amen.*

If you have already given your life to Christ, maybe you need to grow more mature, moving from a small bicycle with training wheels to a new, bigger bike without them. Are you looking for inner transformation in an area of your life? Will you rely on Jesus' power and person today? His Holy Spirit is at work in you to conform you to the image of Christ (Romans 8:29). Jesus lives in you, transforming you so you are becoming like Him. Paul tells us that the Spirit of God transforms us into the image of Christ from glory to glory (2 Corinthians 3:18). Pray this prayer:

> *Lord, fill me with Your Holy Spirit today. I give You this area of my life and ask You to continue Your work in me, making me the woman You want me to be.*

New life. You can't buy it, but you can receive it. And when you receive God's grace gift of newness, get ready for a brand-new adventure of receiving beauty for ashes, riches for poverty, and abundance for every need. Believe it, receive it, and live it. Read on to discover what grace does as God transforms you from an earthbound caterpillar into a soaring butterfly.

IT'S NOT YOUR LIFE

I opened the door of my favorite local bakery and instantly felt better, anticipating some good coffee and great food. I was feeling quite overwhelmed with my responsibilities and had been wallowing in despair for a number of days, wondering about the direction of my life. Once inside the bakery, I spotted one of my pastor friends sipping on his coffee and reading his Bible. I hadn't seen him in months, so I walked over and greeted him with a smile and a warm hello.

He said, "Catherine, how are you? It's so good to see you."

I said, "I'm doing okay. I've been kind of overwhelmed with all my responsibilities. And I've just been wondering what God is doing in my life."

He smiled, "Let me tell you a story."

I said, "Okay," knowing this was going to be good.

"My daughter called me the other day. She said, 'Dad, I'm just not sure what I'm going to do in my life.' Do you know what I said to her?"

"What?" I asked, sensing that I was about to experience an eye-opening truth in this God-ordained appointment.

"I said to my daughter, 'Well, *that's* your problem. It's not your life. It's His life.' She asked me, 'What do you mean?' I said, 'Well, you've been twice given. And I was there to witness both times. First, when you were born, your mother and I gave you to the Lord. And I was there the day you gave your life to Christ. It's not your life; it's His life.'"

I looked at my pastor friend, smiled knowingly, and walked to my table, silently talking with God. *Lord, You got me today! My life is not my own, but Yours—such a simple truth, but deep and profound. Thank You for bringing that pastor to a bakery he never frequents just to remind a simple girl wallowing in pity that I belong to You and that my life is Yours. A metamorphosis has truly taken place. You now live in and through me, and You have the freedom to take me wherever You desire me to go. I am Yours.* That day, in a new way, God set my heart free to love and serve Him.

I remember the first time I realized that Christ lived in me and I belonged to Him. I was studying the book of Romans with an older woman named Thea. For many months, we had discussed each verse, and we had arrived at Romans 6. In that chapter I discovered a life-changing truth. I learned that when I receive Christ and experience the new birth and metamorphosis, I am forever united with Christ. Through Him I experience several things that make my new life in Him possible:

> I have died to sin (6:2).
>
> I am baptized into Christ's death (6:3).
>
> I'm buried with Christ (6:4).
>
> I'm also raised with Christ to newness of life (6:5).
>
> I am united with Christ in death and in the resurrection (6:5).
>
> I am no longer under law, but under grace (6:14).

Because I am united with Christ, I now experience His life. I learned my union with Christ, described so vividly in Romans 6, is the very foundation of my daily experience with Him.

Thea led me further into God's Word, teaching me a few more life-changing truths related to my union with Christ: I no longer live, but Christ lives in me (Galatians 2:20). I thought about the meaning of those words. How could Christ live in me? Christ dwells in my heart through faith (Ephesians 3:17). So my own faith in Jesus appropriates the experience of knowing Christ. Paul describes this experience as a mystery: Christ in me is the hope of glory (Colossians 1:27). And the indwelling Christ *is* a mystery. I cannot possibly understand all the details of how He can live His life in and through me, but I know my body is a temple of the Holy Spirit (1 Corinthians 3:16).

Learning about the Holy Spirit living in me helped me understand how Christ lives His life in and through me. The Holy Spirit's work in us makes such an extraordinary life possible. Christ is my life (Colossians 3:4). Knowing He is my life changed my whole focus. I was no longer concerned about what I wanted to do. Now I wanted to know what Christ wanted to do in and through me. My life was not my own, but His.

These were hefty truths that were filling the heart and mind of such a young girl. I drove home from Thea's house that day thinking, *What does all this mean? I know it makes a difference in me, but I'm not sure how to apply these truths.*

What I first learned that day at Thea's house is known by many as the exchanged life, the crucified life, and the abundant, victorious life of those who are saved by grace. All these precious, vital truths relate directly to the cross of Christ. Most believers, sometime during their journey with the Lord, will catch glimpses of these truths. But not every believer stops long enough to consider the meaning and application of these truths in her life.

These "grace truths" about the exchanged life—Christ living in you (His life for your life)—are essential if you would grow spiritually in the garden of grace. Often, Christians spend years living in the flesh, relying on themselves to serve, grow, and live out their days. And the result is a deep sense of frustration and failure. Many often wonder, *Where's the victory? Where's the abundant life?* The Lord would have you know you no longer belong to yourself, but to Him. He wants you to live in the control and power of His Spirit so He can live in and through you for His glory. You no longer rely on yourself, but on Christ in you. He is the victory, and His life is the abundant life.

✳

Steve McVey prayed for strength after accepting the pastorate of a new church that desperately needed his leadership. Instead, God made him weaker. He described himself after his first year at the new church as "broken and hopeless." He questioned God. "Had God brought me to this church only to set me up for failure? Couldn't He see that I was doing everything I knew how for Him? I couldn't imagine what more He expected from me than my best. And I had done my best. God, what more do You want from me?"[1]

He lay on the floor until almost two in the morning, crying until there were no tears. He looked up, and his eyes fell on a piece of paper sitting on his desk. Someone had given him an article on absolute surrender. On one side was a list of commitments to God. The other side listed items to surrender to God, such as the right to an easy life and certain results. McVey held the paper, as though placed in his hands by God Himself, and prayed down the lists on each side. *Lord, I'm tired of struggling for victory in my own life, and I'm tired of striving for success in my ministry.* Then he prayed prayers of surrender and commitment: *I lay aside everything that gives me a sense of worth. I give You all my efforts to help this church grow. I give You my desire for affirmation, my education and experience.* One after another, he laid down all his rights, all his hopes and desires, and every dream in his heart. Finally, he prayed through the last paragraph on the sheet:

> *I give God permission to do anything He wishes to me, with me,
> in me, or through me that would glorify Him. I once claimed*

> *these rights as mine, but now they belong to God and are under*
> *His control. He can do with them anything He pleases.*[2]

McVey then signed his name to that final prayer of commitment, sensing a life-altering moment. In describing the change in his life, he said, "When I left my office that morning, I didn't want a new program or plan. I wanted only one thing—Him."

McVey experienced a God-ordained moment, just as other grace walkers do when they realize their lives are no longer their own, but Christ's. I believe these moments occur more than once in our lives, for though we may discover a spiritual truth only once, we experiencially *know* it in newer and deeper ways with each season of growth. Here we see the process of spiritual growth, moving from faith to faith (Romans 1:17) and going from strength to strength (Psalm 84:7). Perhaps that's why Steve Mcvey calls our life with Christ a grace *walk.*

> Nothing you have ever done, nothing you could ever do,
> will match the incomparable joy of letting Jesus live His life
> through you. It is what makes the fire of passion burn so
> brightly in new believers. And it is what causes the light of
> contentment to dance in the eyes of mature believers who
> have learned the secret of the Grace Walk.

This walk is a walk with Christ, moment by moment, in the garden of grace, as He lives His life in and through us to touch a lost and hurting world.

No wonder Paul said we are earthen vessels carrying a treasure. The treasure is Christ Himself, who wants to do incredible things in and through you and me. He takes possession of you—all of you. You have died, and your life is hidden with Christ in God (Colossians 3:3). Think about this and what it means practically for you.

Whether you are a wife, a mother, a student, a worker, or a minister, let your prayer be, *Lord, I'm Yours. I no longer live, but You live in me. My life now belongs to You. Do whatever You'd like in and through me.* No wonder Paul said he claimed to talk about nothing but Jesus and Him crucified. For him the preaching of the cross meant that he had new life in Christ. Paul no longer lived, but Christ lived in him. Every day, life was only focused on one person—Christ. What does Jesus want to do today? Where does Jesus want to go?

I remember studying the book of Romans long into the night for a class in seminary. And after studying those truths in such depth, I sensed the Lord was asking me for a new and deeper commitment. Romans 12:1 took on a whole new meaning for me. The words "Present your bodies a living and holy sacrifice" burned in my heart and mind. And in the moments that followed, I got on my face before the Lord and gave Him every part of myself to use in any way He pleased.

Not long after that time of surrender, God entrusted me with the assignment of Quiet Time Ministries. I believe God calls us to new surrenders because of His plans and purposes. Often, times of wrestling and struggle precede great God-moments in our lives. He is bringing us to a place where He can have His way with us and accomplish great and mighty things for His glory. You can know that when you walk in the garden of grace, a time of darkness may precede a moment of glory. Never doubt the high and grand designs of your God. He can be trusted with all of you.

✳

Night had fallen. Would tonight be the night Nicodemus would ask the question burning in his heart? He might not have another opportunity. Jesus was in his village now, and he knew where He was staying. More than anything Nicodemus longed for the fulfillment of prophecy, the coming of a Messiah who would deliver the Jews from Roman rule. He knew what people were saying. "This Jesus does what no other man can do. Is He the Christ, the Messiah?" Nicodemus had heard Jesus teach as no other man taught, speaking as one sent from God. And he could not stop thinking about Jesus' words.

In fact, thinking was one of Nicodemus' more refined skills. He loved to debate about the law so he could understand and keep it. Nicodemus was a religious professional. He could discuss anything concerning God. An expert in the law, he could explain the law to anyone. After all, he was a ruler of the Jews. *I've heard Jesus answer questions in ways I could have never imagined. His wisdom excels any truth I've ever contemplated. I must talk with Jesus,* Nicodemus may have thought. *But no one can know. No one can see. My colleagues hate Jesus and are conspiring against Him even now.*

Now was the time. Compelled, Nicodemus grabbed his cloak and quickly stepped out onto the stone streets. Hurrying to the door of the house he had watched from afar, he thought about what he would say to Jesus. He had spoken to many rulers, but somehow speaking with Jesus felt different. He wasn't afraid, yet he feared. His reverence for Jesus was deeper than his feelings about the law. He just could not fully understand what he felt.

The door opened, and Nicodemus followed some men he had seen before, some of Jesus' disciples, as they led him to a room near the back of the house. Nicodemus reviewed his words in his mind, making sure he could express his questions clearly. Little did he know that Jesus had plans of His own, for Jesus would seek and save those who were lost.

Nicodemus began with words of respect. "Rabbi, we know that You have come from God as a teacher; for no one can do these signs that You do unless God is with him" (John 3:2).

Jesus did not ask Nicodemus for questions. He didn't ask about his wants. He got to the heart of the matter. For He knew Nicodemus, the thinking man, the religious man who claimed to know God. Jesus would show him the way to his true heart's desire.

"Truly, truly, I say to you, unless one is born again he cannot see the kingdom of God."

Nicodemus said to Him, "How can a man be born when he is old?"

Nicodemus clearly didn't understand Jesus' statement. And how could he? This side of the cross, he couldn't understand the astounding transformation, the new spiritual birth, that would be made possible when Jesus was crucified.

Jesus elaborated. He explained as no teacher of the law had ever taught among the Pharisees. His words electrified His hearers. And among them, Nicodemus, a hungry religious ruler of the Jews, listened. "That which is born of the flesh is flesh, and that which is born of the Spirit is spirit. Do not be amazed that I said to you, 'You must be born again.'"

Now Nicodemus was perplexed and completely engaged in conversation with Jesus. "How can these things be?"

Jesus answered and said to him, "Are you the teacher of Israel and do not understand these things?"

Of course, Jesus knew he did not understand. But His words effectively drove home the point to Nicodemus. Jesus knew him through and through. Jesus knew that for all the law Nicodemus debated each day, Nicodemus truly did not know God. Nicodemus knew the law, but he did not know grace.

Now Jesus launched into an in-depth conversation of grace and included some of the most famous words in the Bible.

"As Moses lifted up the serpent in the wilderness, even so must the Son of Man be lifted up; so that whoever believes will in Him have eternal life. For God so loved the world, that He gave His only begotten Son, that whoever believes in Him shall not perish, but have eternal life."

The good news from Jesus in John 3:16 contains the best words anyone can hear. You can't earn eternal life. God gives it. It's a gift. It's all about grace, for grace and truth were realized through Jesus Christ (John 1:17). Grace is necessary even for someone like Nicodemus who knows the law. In his heart of hearts, Nicodemus must have known he couldn't keep the law. No one can keep all the law. Even if people think they are perfect, deep down they know what resides in their hearts. The envy, resentment, and bitterness sometimes boil to the surface for all to see. The sinner needs a Savior. Law meets grace right at the cross. Jesus theologically and practically explained the gospel of grace to Nicodemus that evening. And the new birth He spoke of pointed to a new life—Christ's life in us.

Did this conversation take on new meaning a few years later when Nicodemus, along with Joseph of Arimathea, pulled Jesus' lifeless body off the cross? His hands held grace as few others have. Touching the body of Jesus, crucified on the cross, Nicodemus surely must have remembered those words, "God so loved the world, that He gave His only begotten Son…"

✳

Ian Thomas became a Christian at 13 and decided two years later to serve the Lord for the rest of his life. And so Ian filled his life with numerous activities, all devoted to Christian service. And yet he felt ineffective. Regardless of how hard he worked, nothing seemed to happen in his ministry. Finally one night, he got on his knees, weeping, and cried out to the Lord, "O God, I know that I am saved. I love Jesus Christ. I am perfectly convinced that I am converted. With all my heart I have wanted to serve Thee. I have tried my uttermost and I am a hopeless failure!"[4]

Immediately, verses of Scripture filled his mind. One in particular, Colossians 3:4, stood out to him: "When Christ, who is our life, is revealed, then you also will be revealed with Him in glory." He kept thinking, "Christ, who is our life…life…new life." Suddenly, a huge burden lifted. He realized, "It's not my life. It's Christ's life." It seemed that night as though the Lord was telling him he had been busy trying to do *for* God what only God could do *through* him. Life with Christ was a matter of accepting and acting on the life of Christ in him.

Identification with Christ as your life begins with your identification with Him in His death. The cross is central to the new life in Christ. Jesus spoke of this new life when He said to Nicodemus, "You must be born again." You need to know that your old life ends in Christ's

death on the cross. When you are born again, you experience the resurrection life of Christ, who now lives in you through the indwelling
Holy Spirit.

Elisabeth Elliot, in speaking of the cross in her own life, said, "I saw
that the chance to die, to be crucified with Christ, was not a morbid
thing, but the very gateway to Life." [5]

You might be thinking, *What do I do with these grace truths? I'm
identified with Jesus on the cross. Now He lives in and through me. How
can I apply that to my life in the garden of grace?* The greatest part of
our spiritual growth is to believe God's Word, receive all grace's benefits, and daily live out what we know is true. We believe what is true
about God and about us. Then we receive Christ, His life in us, His
Word, the controlling and empowering Holy Spirit, spiritual gifts, and
God's assignments for our lives of service. The result? Rest—a contentment, peace, assurance, and sense of well-being from Christ. We
enter the rest of Jesus, secure in the everlasting arms of the Lord, and
enjoy Him forever (Deuteronomy 33:27; Hebrews 4:10).

When you realize that your life is *His* life, you know you are not
alone in your circumstance. Your challenges are His, your trials are His,
your obstacles are His...whatever you face, He is also facing because
He now lives in you. And therein lies the victory. Whatever may be
impossible because of your insufficiency is not impossible for Him. He
is an all-sufficient, all-powerful, and victorious overcomer. That's why
He said, "Apart from Me you can do nothing" (John 15:5). Through
the power of the indwelling Holy Spirit, you have everything you need
for everything you face in life because Christ lives in you. You can say,
"I can't, but He can!"

✳

Sitting at a table, I was looking at the plate of food set before me.
I couldn't touch it. I was terrified. I looked out at the women seated
at other tables throughout the room. *There must be at least a thousand*

women here. My heart sank. It was one of the first times I had ever spoken to such a large crowd, and I was afraid. So scared, in fact, that I thought, *Maybe I'll just leave. I'll get in my car and go.* But my fleeting thoughts of escape could not overcome my excitement about sharing the message God had placed in my heart. A wrestling match ensued between two wills—mine and the Lord's.

Eventually, promises of God's strength flooded my mind. "I can do all things through Him who strengthens me" (Philippians 4:13). "You will receive power" (Acts 1:8). I had heard enough from the faithful Holy Spirit, who was bringing tremendous words from the Bible to encourage me and remind me of His strength in me. Silently I prayed, *Lord, I'm going to step up on that stage no matter what. Even if I freak out and fail, I'm still going up there and giving my message. Even if I'm afraid, even if I'm weak, I'm going for it. I'm relying on You, Lord, to be my strength and to minister to this group of women through me.*

As I walked up the stairs to the stage, a warm peace enveloped my heart. A calm settled in my soul. I preached my heart out. As I shared my testimony and the words God had helped me prepare, I was astounded at the strength I felt standing there. *Thank You, Lord, for living in me and loving others through me,* I prayed silently as I shared the message with these women. I've never forgotten that moment when I launched out by faith in what I knew to be true and experienced Christ living in me and strengthening me to speak out for Him.

✳

Because we are in Christ, we have received every spiritual blessing in Him (Ephesians 1:3). We already have everything we desire. So now we need to believe, receive, and live in light of God's gracious blessings.

Sometimes the greatest nuggets of teaching are hidden away in books long out of print. One of the best paragraphs I have ever read on grace and Christ's life in me is in William R. Newell's book on

Romans. He lists "things which gracious souls discover." In his short conclusions, Newell shows us how to apply the spiritual blessings of our life with Christ in the garden of grace:

"Grace, once bestowed, is not withdrawn: for God knew all the human exigencies beforehand; His action was independent of them, not dependent upon them." Now I know God's offer of grace is fully dependent on Him, not me. I am free to enjoy God's gifts—all of them.

"To believe, and to consent to be loved while unworthy, is the great secret." Spiritual growth occurs when I agree to let God love me even though I can do nothing to earn His grace and compassion.

"To expect to be blessed, though realizing more and more lack of worth." Grace walkers know the blessing of God, yet they realize they've done nothing to deserve His gifts.

"There being no cause in the creature why grace should be shown, the creature must be brought off from trying to give cause to God for His care." I learn that I cannot earn my way to God's acceptance. I don't have to find reasons for God to love me. I have His love now before I have done anything.

"He has been accepted in Christ, who is his standing. He is not on probation." What joy and freedom I experience when I realize my acceptance depends on the works of Christ, not my own inadequate, deficient abilities.

"As to his life past, it does not exist before God: he died at the cross, and Christ is His Life." I gain a new understanding of the cross and its implication for my present life. I am forgiven. And if I truly died at the cross and possess new life in Christ, the old life is dead and gone.

"To refuse to make 'resolutions' and 'vows'; for that is to trust in the flesh." I need to learn to trust in Christ's life in me rather than self.

"To 'hope to be better' (hence acceptable) is to fail to see yourself in Christ only." Seeing myself in Christ implies a whole new view of life. I rely on Him for everything, including my acceptance by God and my character transformation.

"To be disappointed with yourself is to have believed in yourself." When I first read this, I memorized the words. I realized my great need to rely on Christ for every action, every good deed.

"To be discouraged is unbelief—as to God's purpose and plan of blessing for you." I can never give up because Christ lives in me. What a promise!

"To be proud, is to be blind! For we have no standing before God, in ourselves." There is no room for pride, for Christ is the source of our life.

These powerful grace truths flow out of Romans 6 and are the practical ramifications of knowing Christ is my life and lives in and through me. Brother Yun understood these gracious truths when he said this to his wife, Deling:

> We are absolutely nothing. We have nothing to be proud about. We have no abilities and nothing to offer God. The fact he chooses to use us is only due to his grace. It has nothing to do with us. If God should choose to raise up others for his purpose and never to use us again we would have nothing to complain about.[6]

These are secrets to growing spiritually deep. You are not the one doing the work—Christ is at work in you!

One of the great results of your identification with Christ is the glory of God shining in you through Christ. You are a vessel housing the very glory of Christ in you. Paul says that the light of His glory shines in our hearts (2 Corinthians 4:6).

Some never realize Christ is their life. May you grow in the garden, receive this grace gift, and know this powerful truth as you have never known it before. On whom are you relying? Yourself or Christ? It's His life. Jesus is issuing a call for death to self and life in Him. He invites us to the life of the cross when He says, "If anyone wishes to come after Me, he must deny himself, and take up his cross daily and follow

Me" (Luke 9:23). The life of the cross means we, like Paul, "die daily" (1 Corinthians 15:31) in that we appropriate anew, by faith, the fact that we no longer live, but Christ lives in us. Then, with eyes fixed on Him (Hebrews 12:1-3), we look to Him for His desires, His ways, His purposes...His life. Truly, His life is manifested in our bodies, and daily we carry the treasure of Christ Himself in our bodies, which are earthen vessels (2 Corinthians 4:7-10). God's gracious gift of Christ in you...believe it, receive it, and live it.

Today, dear friend, do you realize the importance of the cross in your life? Do you realize that if your life is no longer your own, but His, then there is no room for fret or worry? Jesus surely knows what He wants to do in you and where He wants to go. When you follow Him, He will lead you every step of the way. Let's discover together all we receive as we walk with Jesus and grow deep in the garden of grace.

> Not I, but Christ, be honoured, loved, exalted,
> Not I, but Christ, be seen, be known and heard;
> Not I, but Christ, in every look and action,
> Not I, but Christ, in every thought and word.
>
> Not I, but Christ, in lowly silent labour,
> Not I, but Christ, in humble earnest toil;
> Christ, only Christ, no show, no ostentation;
> Christ, none but Christ, the gatherer of the spoil.
>
> Christ, only Christ! no idle word e'er falling,
> Christ, only Christ; no needless bustling sound;
> Christ, only Christ; no self-important bearing;
> Christ, only Christ; no trace of "I" be found.
>
> Not I, but Christ, my every need supplying,
> Not I, but Christ, my strength and health to be;
> Not I, but Christ, for spirit, soul and body,
> Christ, only Christ, live even Thy life in me.

Christ, only Christ, ere long will fill my vision;
Glory excelling, soon, full soon I'll see
Christ, only Christ, my every wish fulfilling—
Christ, only Christ, my all in all to be.

Oh, to be saved from myself, dear Lord,
Oh, to be lost in Thee,
Oh, that it may be no more I,
But Christ that lives in me.[7]

6

BEAUTY FOR ASHES

Sheri Rose Shepherd checked into a hotel, hopeless and desperate to ease the heartache in her empty soul. She could not go on like this any longer. Battling depression and bulimia, she cried herself to sleep every night. Unwilling to continue this pattern of defeat and failure, she was going to end her life with a bottle of sleeping pills. What an unlikely scenario for a young woman who described herself as having everything that should have meant happiness and fulfillment.

> I was no longer addicted to drugs, I had lost sixty pounds,
> and I owned my own business. I had money, success, beauty
> titles, boyfriends, nice clothes, and people's approval for
> all I had overcome. I drove a nice car and had a calendar
> full of appointments for places to go and people to see...
> On the outside I looked like I had it all together, but on
> the inside I was falling apart. I felt empty and alone even
> when I was in a crowd of people. I could not find any-
> thing or anyone to fill that deep lonely place in my heart.
> I wanted to die.[1]

Time stood still as Sheri Rose contemplated her impending death. Looking at the sleeping pills, ready to end it all, her mind turned to

God. *He's my last hope,* she thought. And so she took a chance and cried out to God, and God heard Sheri Rose's cry and rescued her. She felt surrounded by the presence of God and filled with His love and peace. *Now I know I'm not alone,* she thought, with a new realization of the presence of God.

That night, Sheri Rose received a beautiful crown from her Lord, the crown of everlasting life. He showered her with gifts of His grace, and they turned out to be just what she had been longing for her whole life: love, joy, peace, and a reason for living. In describing her experience, Sheri Rose says, "The King welcomed me into His family as His much-loved daughter."

Ten years later, Sheri Rose stood on a stage of another kind. Bright lights were shining into her eyes, preventing her from looking into the faces of the 2000 people in the audience. Standing on that stage was a miracle and a true testimony to all God had done in her life. The master of ceremonies received the envelope with the name of the winner inside. Then came the moment for the grand announcement.

"The 1994 Mrs. United States of America is...Sheri Rose Shepherd!"

With overwhelming joy, Sheri Rose cried as the crown was placed on her head. Cameras flashed. The audience applauded. She celebrated her victory with the women there in Las Vegas who had become her friends.

Later, as she walked to her hotel room and laid the crown on a table, she thought about her Lord, who had given her a crown of another kind. And she knew, in that moment, there was really no comparison between earthly crowns and the crown of beauty given by the King of kings and Lord of lords.

✳

True beauty resides in the heart. Our adornment is not only external but also in the "hidden person of the heart" (1 Peter 3:3). How is our heart adorned with beauty? Very simply, when Christ lives in you, He makes you beautiful. You are now clothed with Christ (Galatians 3:27). God gives you the gift of spiritual beauty and a new position. You are in Christ, and Christ is in you, so He is always present with you. So when you walk down the path with Jesus in the garden of grace, you discover He has given you Himself, transforming you with His beauty, His holiness, and His glory.

What does Christ's presence mean for you? Your beauty is the fulfillment of God's promise through His prophet Isaiah of a "crown of beauty instead of ashes" (Isaiah 61:3 NIV). The presence of Christ in you is a crown of beauty, declaring to the world that you belong to Him. You are His princess bride, so to speak.

If you have entered into a forever relationship with the Lord, then there is more to you than meets my eyes, my friend. Once you belong to Christ, you are His forever. And your beauty, true and real beauty, is of utmost importance to Him. You are going to discover, as you walk in the garden of grace, that your Lord spares nothing to give you everything you need to shine brightly in His kingdom. Will you believe it? Will you receive it? Will you live it? Then you will grow and experience a new walk in the garden of grace.

Have you ever watched a beauty pageant? Once the winner is announced, a crown is placed on her head. She may even wear a beautiful robe and hold a bouquet or a scepter. She is queen for the day and the star of the show. There is no doubt as to who has won the contest. And the woman wins because the judges determined that she is the most beautiful.

In your case, you are not chosen because you were the best or brightest, but because God loves you. Then you are given your true beauty in Christ, and you shine with His glory. The more you walk in the garden of grace, the more beautiful you discover you are. You learn, by faith, looking through your Bible glasses, the truth about yourself. When you see yourself as God sees you—in Christ—you grow deep in the garden of grace.

In Ezekiel 16, we see what God's grace really looks like when He gives beauty to the undeserving and unlovely because of sheer love. God describes, in minute detail, His actions toward His people, Israel. He was passing by one day and saw His people, the least of many and the most needy. He covered them, entered into a covenant, and made them His very own. Now the people were His. So how does God treat a people who become His own? In Ezekiel 16 we discover the truth.

God washed them and anointed them with oil. He clothed them with embroidered cloth and put sandals of porpoise skin on their feet. He wrapped them with fine linen and silk. He adorned them with fine jewelry—bracelets on their hands, a necklace around their neck, a ring in their nostril, earrings in their ears, and a beautiful crown on their head. He gave them fine flour, honey, and oil to eat. He made them "exceedingly beautiful and advanced to royalty." They were known among the nations for their beauty, which was made perfect because of the splendor of God bestowed on them.

Sadly, the people rejected God. In spite of His loving care and kindness, they refused to give God any attention and instead chose to go their own way and worship other gods.

Why does God take the time to give us so many details about His care for the people of Israel? I believe God wants us to understand His love and mercy, given as gifts of grace. When we truly know how exquisitely He beautifies us, in every detail, we will live for Him and honor Him in everything we do. And perhaps we won't forget who we are or whose we are.

✳

What happens when a woman lives as the person she has now become? A woman named Esther (also known as Hadassah) shows us the way. She was an orphan girl, adopted by her cousin Mordecai. And her life might have continued on into obscurity had Queen Vashti not decided one day, in pride and arrogance, to defy her husband, King

Ahasuerus. Thus ended the position and power of Queen Vashti. The king's attendants advised, "Let beautiful young virgins be sought for the king…let the young lady who pleases the king be queen in place of Vashti" (Esther 2:2-4).

Esther was taken to the king's palace along with many other young women to undergo a yearlong beautification process. When Esther entered the presence of the king, she found favor and kindness. He placed a crown on her head and made her queen in place of Vashti. And so, within a year, Esther moved from orphan to royalty, from obscurity to renown, from plainness to lavish beauty. Why would God move a simple Jewish girl into such a glorious place? He knew that Esther would be His woman for just such a time as this.

An official named Haman hated the Jews and devised an evil plan. He convinced the king to issue a decree slaughtering all Jews on a particular day. Mordecai learned of the plan and appealed to Esther, urging her to use her position and beg for the king's mercy. Such an audacious request was a risk. No one could approach the king without a summons. The only hope was the king's decision to hold out the golden scepter and spare the person's life.

Esther was faced with a choice. Should she risk her life, go to the king, and hope that he would spare her? She responded, "If I perish, I perish." She assumed her position as queen and boldly approached the king. Her actions were rewarded as he held out the golden scepter. She exposed the evil actions of Haman, and her people were saved.

Esther is an example of how God chooses the least likely, brings them into positions of power and influence, makes them beautiful, puts crowns on their heads, and uses them for His high and holy purposes. Every day you need to wear your royal robes and live in the presence of your King, who is your Lord. Be bold, like Esther, and walk like the woman you are in Christ. Always remember you are a princess, and you are His bride, soon to be presented to Him in glory. You are chosen by God, and holy and beloved (Colossians 3:12). You are a child of God, a saint, and a citizen of God's kingdom (Ephesians 2:19). You are a member of Christ's body, the church (Ephesians 5:23). Twentieth-century theologian Lewis Sperry Chafer explains, "A believer is a citizen of heaven, and therefore in the present world he is an ambassador, a stranger, a pilgrim, and a witness against the evils of the cosmos and Satan."[2]

In light of these truths, you cannot walk like a mere woman, as the apostle Paul pointed out to the Corinthian church (1 Corinthians 3:3-4). You cannot live a fleshly life, harboring jealousy, strife, self-pity, or despair. You are now royalty. You are spiritual. As a child of the King, you have been given all the rights and privileges that belong to Jesus Christ, for you are united with Him. And so, in the garden of grace, you live like who you are—a beautiful princess. Affirm His grace in your life today. Believe it, receive it, and live it.

But you may say, "Well, I just don't see it." Friend, just give God time. Walk with Him in the garden of grace for a while. The more you walk in the garden of grace with your Lord, the more you will see the beauty of the Lord shining in your life. This life you live is not about something you do. Your true life encompasses the person of Christ, who lives in and through you as you are filled with His Spirit. You will marvel when you witness His love, His kindness, His joy, and His compassion shining through you and touching the lives of others.

How then can you begin this process of being filled with the Spirit, giving Jesus control of your life, and being empowered and transformed? Pray by faith, *Lord, fill me with your Holy Spirit.* If He convicts you of sin, confess it. If He asks you to hand Him a burden, give it over to Him. If He leads you in an unusual direction, respond by saying, *Yes, Lord.* And then you will begin to see Him shine in your life, and you will wear garments of beauty as you walk with Him.

I love Max Lucado's description of how we become beautiful and are clothed with Christ:

> For years I owned an elegant suit complete with coat, trousers, even a hat. I considered myself quite dapper in the outfit

and was confident others agreed. The pants were cut from the cloth of my good works, sturdy fabric of deeds done and projects completed. Some studies here, some sermons there. Many people complimented my trousers, and I confess, I tended to hitch them up in public so people would notice them. The coat was equally impressive. It was woven together from my convictions. Each day I dressed myself in deep feelings of religious fervor. My emotions were quite strong. So strong, in fact, that I was often asked to model my cloak of zeal in public gatherings to inspire others. Of course I was happy to comply. While there I'd also display my hat, a feathered cap of knowledge. Formed with my own hands from the fabric of personal opinion, I wore it proudly. *Surely God is impressed with my garments,* I often thought. Occasionally I strutted into his presence so he could compliment the self-tailored wear. He never spoke. *His silence must mean admiration,* I convinced myself. But then my wardrobe began to suffer. The fabric of my trousers grew thin. My best works started coming unstitched. I began leaving more undone than done, and what little I did was nothing to boast about. *No problem,* I thought. *I'll work harder.* But working harder *was* a problem. There was a hole in my coat of convictions. My resolve was threadbare. A cold wind cut into my chest. I reached up to pull my hat down firmly, and the brim ripped off in my hands. Over a period of a few months, my wardrobe of self-righteousness completely unraveled. I went from tailored gentlemen's apparel to beggars' rags. Fearful that God might be angry at my tattered suit, I did my best to stitch it together and cover my mistakes. But the cloth was so worn. And the wind was so icy. I gave up. I went back to God. (Where else could I go?) On a wintry Thursday afternoon, I stepped into his presence, not for applause, but for warmth. My prayer was feeble.

"I feel naked."

"You are. And you have been for a long time." What he did next I'll never forget. "I have something to give you," he said. He gently removed the remaining threads and then picked up a robe, a regal robe, the clothing of his own goodness. He wrapped it around my shoulders. His words to me were tender. *"My son, you are now clothed with Christ"* (see Galatians 3:27).[3]

What kind of clothes do you wear as you live in the world and walk in the garden of grace? Your clothing is inner, spiritual, in the heart. Paul shows us in Colossians 3:12-17 the true appearance of our garments when Christ is shining within. These qualities in you make you truly beautiful in God's eyes.

First, you are to put on a heart of compassion. Compassion is tenderness and mercy expressed toward others. You demonstrate with your actions that you're not all about business. You also have heart. You have within you the power to choose compassion because Christ is now living in you. You will find His compassion bubbling up within you at times for no apparent reason when Christ is at work in you.

We see the tenderness of Christ when He raised Lazarus from the dead. When all around Him were weeping, brokenhearted over the loss of one they loved, Jesus wept (John 11:35). Only one with compassion, a tender heart easily melted and touched, can weep with those who weep. Christ in you will give you this beauty of a tender, warm heart for others.

Then, put on a heart of kindness. This grace response gives a blessing to undeserving people. It's the fine art of being nice instead of mean to someone else. Jesus demonstrated kindness one day when He walked by a tree, looked up at a man sitting on a branch, and said, "Zaccheus! I'm coming to your house today!" Zaccheus hurried down and excitedly led Jesus to his home.

This kindness singles out people in a crowd and pours out a blessing.

When Christ shines through, He helps you notice invisible people, those who have no advocate but need just a drop of water to quench their thirst. You will see others as you have never seen them before. Don't be surprised to find ideas for acts of kindness welling up in your heart and mind. Get ready for this new kindness adventure as the Lord leads you.

Then, as the Lord's princess, your beauty is seen even more clearly when you put on humility. The greatest picture of humility is Christ's willingness to lay aside His heavenly rights, come to earth, and die on the cross for our sins (Philippians 2:5-11). Christ's humility will shine in you, making you eager to lay aside your own rights. God can use you in any arena when nothing is beneath you. Clothed in humility, you become approachable, affable, and available.

Another aspect of your true beauty is gentleness. This inner grace of the soul brings calmness toward God, accepts His dealings, and trusts in His goodness. Those who are gentle act in kindness toward others regardless of their actions or attitudes. Jesus' gentleness was on display when a leper came to Him and asked for healing.

"Lord, if You are willing, You can make me clean" (Matthew 8:2).

Was Jesus willing? Does He desire to do good to others? What is Jesus really like? The leper's request seemed to encompass a multitude of questions about Jesus' character. But Jesus responded with real gentleness toward this outcast who had no hope for the future without divine intervention.

"Jesus stretched out His hand and touched him." No other person would ever touch a leper, especially in first-century Palestine. Yet with a gentle action, Jesus touched the leper and said, "I am willing; be cleansed."

How often do we need the gentle touch of Jesus? And how much more does the world need the spirit of gentleness present in Christ alone? You will discover numerous opportunities to let the gentleness of Christ shine in you, especially when you encounter angry and cross tempers. Choose Christ's gentleness in the power of God's Spirit and watch His beauty draw others to Himself.

You are also beautiful because of the patience of Christ shining in your heart. Real patience bears injustices without revenge or retaliation. Christ was supremely patient with His own accusers. When He was brought to trial, Pilate and Herod questioned Him. The Roman soldiers mocked Him. Jesus, as commander of the armies of heaven, could have destroyed all His enemies in seconds. Yet He bore their insults to achieve a greater result—paying the penalty for our sins that we might be forgiven and inherit eternal life. When you choose patience through the power of the Holy Spirit, Christ's patience in you will win over antagonistic people in your life. Even an unbelieving or rebellious husband can be "won without a word" by the beautiful behavior of a godly woman (1 Peter 3:1-5).

Another aspect of your inner beauty is the ability to bear with another person. Christ in you endures or "puts up with" errors and weaknesses in others. This endurance is beautiful to the Lord, who demonstrated endurance toward His own disciples. Think of the time when the disciples began arguing among themselves about who was the greatest (Luke 9:46-48). Jesus could have admonished them. Instead, He taught them a lesson about true greatness—receiving a child in His name. As you walk in the garden of grace, filled with the Holy Spirit, weaknesses in others become opportunities to minister the endurance of Christ.

Real beauty shines in your forgiveness of others, especially for those closest to you. Sometimes we demand the most from those we love. Jesus teaches us the beauty of forgiveness in His words on the cross: "Father, forgive them, for they do not know what they are doing" (Luke 23:34). You may not have the strength to forgive, but you can draw on Christ's strength in you. And in Him, you will find enough forgiveness for whatever wrong you or another has suffered.

After you are clothed with all these beautiful garments, there is one quality you wear above all others—the love of Christ. In fact, love is the thread holding all of the other garments together. Love is the smile you always wear, compelling you to reach out to needy, desperate souls in the world. Jesus loves even the sinner, the lost, and those whom others would call despicable. He loves the unlovely and unworthy. Love sent Him to the cross, kept Him on the cross, and achieved your eternal salvation. And this same love beats in your heart through Christ. Perhaps there is no greater quality that makes you more beautiful than the love of God shed abroad in your heart (Romans 5:5). Love always wins the day and breaks down otherwise unbreakable barriers between people. The greatest attribute of the grace-filled believer is love (1 Corinthians 13:13).

When the Lord looks at you, He sees every facet of your beauty shining like a diamond, for He looks past your outer appearance and into your heart. And there, in your heart, Christ reigns supreme, ruling with peace and making you more and more beautiful every day as He works in you. And thankfully so, for time marches on, and youthful skin becomes lined and creased with each passing year. Regardless of how much antiaging lotion we may apply, our outer appearance is going to change. Let's get real about aging—before too long, if we live long enough, we're all going to be old according to the world's standards. Yet we are becoming more beautiful on the inside moment by moment according to the Lord. And though the outer body is temporal, our inner beauty is eternal (2 Corinthians 4:16-18).

Hollywood offers the counterfeit view of beauty and value. Many women in the movie industry find their careers have ended by the time they're 40. But in God's economy, your best years could follow your forties and fifties. Kay Arthur began Precept Ministries in her late thirties and continues to lead it today in her seventies. Corrie ten Boom ministered on into her eighties, influencing thousands of lives as a result. Ocie Bard, in her nineties, ministers to the women at our church. A heart beating for the Lord is valuable forever in God's kingdom.

My friend Nancy Stafford is seriously gorgeous and one of the former stars of the television series *Matlock*. She shares an illustrative story about Hollywood's version of beauty. At the age of 44, Nancy auditioned for a part in a TV movie as a fortysomething mother. She nailed the audition and was excited about the potential role. She called her agent, who informed her that the director thought she looked 55! What a low blow for Nancy. She thought, "Well…fifty-five isn't so bad. Just not yet!"[4] Well, as her friend, I'm telling you that Nancy looks as though she is in her early thirties, maybe even younger. The director had no clue about age and even less ability to assess beauty.

I first met Nancy at one of our Women of Revival conferences. I connected with her and saw not only her outer beauty but also her heart on fire for the Lord. Nancy shares her secret to inner beauty in *Beauty by the Book:*

> Remember: Christ bought your identity. He has freed you from the tyranny of other people's expectations and unshackled you from the bonds of comparisons. Your identity isn't determined by *Vogue* magazine, Victoria's Secret, or Calvin Klein, and you don't have to try to meet the unreasonable, attainable standards of the culture. You are unique in every way. So resist the idea of living someone else's idea of what you should look like.[5]

I resonate with Nancy's words about the importance of letting Christ give us true beauty and a new identity. Living day by day as the Lord's beautiful princess requires a bold faith because people and circumstances can make you forget who you are. And so you will find that God trains your faith in the garden of grace. Your faith is tested when the truth about your identity in Christ is challenged by a contradicting feeling or experience.

Probably my most difficult times have come when I did not meet someone else's expectations. We can give our very best, but sometimes our efforts fall short, and the results other people hoped for never materialize. Sometimes a person's expectations for us are unrealistic and outside of God's plan. Maybe God has something even greater in mind than the original expectation. Other times, I find that God is training me to look higher, learn something new, and reach beyond anything I've ever done before.

In these times, I get back to the basics, draw near to God, and ask Him for perspective. First, I remind myself of my relationship with Christ. I belong to Him. I am united with Him. It's His life, not mine. Then I remember I am a child of the King, a princess, and part of the bride of Christ, the church. I am royalty. My beauty is in the heart, and my inner life with Christ is of primary importance. Once again, I put on the clothing of royalty and ask the Lord to help me walk in the garden of grace and live like His princess. Finally, I pray that He will control and empower me with His Spirit, making me the woman He wants me to be. I ask Him to grow me spiritually and give me insight and wisdom in my challenging situation, whatever it may be.

After becoming a Christian, Sheri Rose Shepherd was sitting at a table with her husband's Bible professors and their wives. One of the women said loudly enough for all to hear, "I heard you were fat, Jewish, and on drugs. How did you *ever* become a Christian?"

All eyes were on Sheri Rose, and she was compelled to share her testimony even though she felt like running out of the room. But that night led to the beginning of her speaking ministry. The same woman who humiliated her later invited her to share her testimony with 400 women's ministry leaders. Now, Sheri Rose encourages people to never doubt God.

> He has chosen you and me to be His princesses, and we need to take Him at His Word...We need to walk with confidence in the King, not in our self. If we truly want our lives to matter for eternity, then we better start acting and living like His princesses or we will miss our crowning moment."[6]

Do you realize how beautiful you really are in Christ? Do you know you are the Lord's princess? When I was a little girl, I used to dream I was a princess from another kingdom. I never knew then that my dream would come true. But Jesus crowns me with His beauty and even desires my beauty (Psalm 45:11). Someday, we will see the face of our bridegroom. He will wipe every tear from our eyes. Clothed in glory and made ready as a bride for her husband, we will be presented to Jesus. His name will be on our foreheads, and we will see His face. And we will reign together forever and ever. Hold these truths close to your heart, dear friend, and be encouraged that He has given you His beauty for your ashes.

7

RICHES FOR POVERTY

What was she to do now? What can a 19-year-old woman with two children, a failed marriage, and no means of income do to survive the Depression years? Mary Crowley was accustomed to heartache and challenge. Her mother died when she was 18 months old, and she had lived with different family members until she married at 17.

The one bright light was her grandmother, who had taught her that God was personal and cared for her. Mary learned that Jesus loved her and wanted to be with her. At 13, she committed her life to Christ and regarded Him as her best friend. She trusted Christ and used to look often at a sign over her mirror that read, "Jesus never fails, and Jesus never fails *me*." Though she was poor, she became rich in her relationship with Christ. She relied on Him to lead her through her hopeless situation.

Her grandmother used to say, "When things happen to you, you can lose only if you react to them rather than use the experience to progress…Don't live in *if only* land, Mary."

Everything about her situation seemed to work against her. She had no formal training and very little education. But she had God, and more importantly, God had her. Mary's relationship with God was enough to sustain her.

With Jesus as her best friend, she ventured out in the business world in a time when only a few jobs were available for the thousands searching for work. Walking up and down the streets in Sherman, Texas, she evaluated the stores. What store was most impressive and would provide the best opportunity? Finally she settled on a department store. Dressed in her best outfit, with a big smile, she walked in and said confidently, "I have chosen you to be my employer."

The manager, impressed with her approach, said, "I'll give you a one-day trial. If you do well, you're hired."

She outsold the other employees and was given a full-time position. God used that first job to develop Mary's shrewd business sense in preparation for His future plans for her.

She attended Southern Methodist University, studying accounting for a higher-paying job. She worked for an insurance company and attended school even though she struggled with insomnia. She continued to trust God, praying, *Lord, You know I've got to get my rest. You worry about these problems. You're going to be up all night anyway.*

Following her studies, she became an accountant for a furniture store. Though she worked in an office, she loved the sales floor. She discovered a special interest in home accessories and often quizzed customers about their desires.

In 1948, she married David Crowley, a man she had fallen in love with while working for the insurance company. While working as an accountant, she met Mary Kay Eckman, who later founded Mary Kay Cosmetics. Mary Eckman was working for Stanley Home Products, a home party sales company, and recruited Mary Crowley to join her. She then sold home products for World Gift and managed a staff of 500.

Brewing in her mind was an idea for a brand-new company. But it would mean starting from scratch. She had no capital but a big God. She said, "God saved me from the deadly, crippling diseases of self-pity and resentment. He gave me the courage and determination to start all over again. The result was that my business came into being.

Out of this I learned that when God opens doors, you get up and go through them."[1]

With the full support of her husband, Mary incorporated Home Interiors and Gifts in 1957. It began with her working 80 hours a week and shipping home decorative items out of her garage. Within five years, her company earned $1 million dollars in sales. She believed no one could out-give God, so she gave 10 percent of her income to the Lord. She held to God's promise in Malachi 3:10, believing He pours out blessings when people give with joy from the heart. Mary always gave the credit for her business success to the Lord. Her business operated on a cash basis with virtually no debt. In 1983, her company celebrated its twenty-fifth anniversary with $400 million in sales and a profit of $20 million.

God used Mary Crowley in thousands of people's lives. She was invited to the White House in 1977 as one of only 20 business leaders asked to meet with President Carter. She won the Horatio Alger Award with her rags-to-riches story, and she served on the boards of the American Cancer Society and the Billy Graham Evangelistic Association. She received two honorary doctorate degrees.

During her life, Mary suffered two bouts of cancer, yet she clung to God. Her focus was singular, with her eyes fixed on God and God alone. She loved to "brag on" God: "In this age of what I call 'distractomania,' there are so many things horning in to distract each of us. These things distract us from our chief aim in life. God created us to have fellowship with Him."[2]

Early in her life, after reading the account of Deborah in Judges 4, Mary personalized what she had learned. *I wonder what God could do with Mary Crowley? I want to give Him a chance.*

What was Mary's secret? Her wealth did not reside in money or possessions, but in God, who had given her spiritual riches for her bankrupt soul at 13. She applied the words of Jeremiah 9:23-24, which hung on the wall of the chapel at her home: "'Let not a wise man boast of his wisdom, and let not the mighty man boast of his might, let not a rich man boast of his riches; but let him who boasts boast of this, that he understands and knows Me, that I am the LORD who exercises lovingkindness, justice and righteousness on earth; for I delight in these things,' declares the LORD."

✳

How do you measure your wealth—in dollars and cents or according to the gifts of God's grace? In the garden of grace, you are given the gift of spiritual wealth and the corresponding provision for all your needs. You are rich in Christ whether you have a million dollars or one dollar. Mary Crowley, a wealthy women in her day, regarded Christ as her best friend and her greatest gift. She said, "When I realized what it cost Him to redeem me, then I fully realized my worth."[3] Your worth never depends on your earthly possessions but on Christ alone. As you continue on in your walk with Christ in the garden of grace, you grow taller when you discover He has replaced your poverty with His riches. Affirm God's gracious gift in your life of His wealth for your poverty. Believe it, receive it, and live it.

Does everyone who knows Christ become a multimillionaire? No, but real wealth in the garden of grace is not measured in money or possessions. In fact, according to James, money can actually be a source of trouble if held in the wrong attitude and regarded with the wrong perspective (James 1:9-11). Money becomes trouble when *you* no longer have *it—it* has *you*.

When you wear your Bible glasses, looking at wealth and possessions from God's point of view through His Word, then you realize His grace has made you rich beyond your wildest imagination. What then is yours in Christ?

God has authorized you to receive a glorious inheritance that can never be taken away from you. Temporal wealth and possessions can vanish very quickly, but your inheritance is imperishable and undefiled (1 Peter 1:4). Your wealth is reserved in heaven for you. But you are given a pledge of your inheritance, a down payment, as a promise of things to come—the Holy Spirit, the firstfruits of a rich glory you will experience in heaven. The Spirit lives in you and seals you in Christ, thus making you secure in Him (Ephesians 1:13-14) and promising you forgiveness and eternal life. No one can touch your magnificent inheritance. Regardless of what you endure on earth during your brief stay here, your future inheritance is secure and waiting for you.

Your wealth in the Holy Spirit includes the fruit of love, joy, peace, patience, kindness, goodness, faithfulness, gentleness, and self-control (Galatians 5:22-23). Such qualities make you richer than any billion-aire on earth who does not know Christ. The Holy Spirit gives you power to live the Christian life here on earth (Acts 1:8; Colossians 1:11). No amount of education or earthly possessions can match the power given by the Holy Spirit.

In Christ you are given the riches of wisdom, righteousness, sancti-fication, and redemption. Such gifts can never be bought with money; they can only be received by grace through faith. Wisdom gives you the ability to apply the truth of the Word in your life. Solomon could have received anything he wanted from God, yet he asked for wisdom. God honored his choice and gave him more besides. Righteousness is right standing with God, made possible only in Christ. Sanctification means you are made holy and set apart for God, something you could never become on your own. Finally, God redeemed you from the slave market of sin through the blood of Christ. You have been set free from the law of sin and death. Your sins are forgiven. Such a purchase is made possible only by the gracious gift of His Son. You can't buy freedom from sin, but you can receive redemption through Christ.

You no longer live in the domain of darkness, but have been trans-ferred to the kingdom of Christ (Colossians 1:13). You now live under the reign, rule, and authority of Christ and enjoy the benefits of His kingdom. These benefits, poured out on those who are poor in spirit, include a future home in the eternal kingdom of heaven, a place Christ is preparing for you Himself (Matthew 5:3; John 14:2-3).

In Christ, you are given fellowship with God, brought near by His blood, and granted precious, blessed access to Him (Ephesians 2:13-18). Your relationship with God is something no one can touch. Just think, you can run to God anytime you like because of Christ.

In Christ, you are adopted into the family of God and given privileges of a child of God (Ephesians 1:5). You are like a prodigal who has come home to your Father. He welcomes you with open arms, longing to give you every benefit as His child.

In Christ, His grace is lavished on you (Ephesians 1:7-8). That means God keeps pouring out benefit after benefit—rich expressions of grace. Just when you think you've used up all God has given you, He pours out a new expression of love. God's grace only knows one expression—extravagant, overflowing abundance.

You are wealthy in your intimacy with God through Christ. Your true knowledge of Him gives you everything you need for life and godliness (2 Peter 1:3), making you rich indeed. Men and women spend lifetimes trying to put their lives together. In your intimate relationship with Christ, you have everything you need for life.

You are wealthy because of the "riches of His glory" poured out on you, a vessel of mercy (Romans 9:23). Just think, you carry the glory of Christ in you every day!

Finally, you are wealthy because you are given the promises of God (2 Peter 1:4). Peter calls God's promises "precious and magnificent"; precious because they are more valuable than any earthly possession, and magnificent because they are strong enough to handle and help in any circumstance of life. The Word of God, filled with the promises of God, makes you a spiritual multimillionaire. Every promise is given to you as a check, waiting to be cashed in the bank of heaven. Once you cash a check, you have the privilege of watching to see how God will fulfill His promise in your life. The promises of God afford you a wealth the world will never know, for they breathe real hope into your heart.

The world's counterfeits of spiritual wealth in Christ are money and possessions. Worldly wealth without Christ makes one poor indeed, for it only lasts a little while. People who do not know Christ live in poverty, for they are separate from Christ, excluded from covenant promises, without hope and without God in the world (Ephesians 2:12).

But you, living in the garden of grace, now may trust God's promises and receive your riches in Christ instead of spiritual poverty. Jesus invites us to lay up our treasure in heaven. If you know Christ, you can accumulate spiritual treasure regardless of how much money you have on earth. You can enjoy the Holy Spirit's control and power right now. Draw near to God and experience blessed fellowship with Him, moment by moment. And cash in on God's promises every day, watching God at work in His time as He carries out His purposes in your life. And walk in hope, knowing one day you will enjoy every future benefit waiting in heaven for you.

✳

Lydia was confident about her business in Philippi. She enjoyed her profession of selling the famed purple cloth manufactured by the guilds of Thyatira. She had chosen Philippi because of its busy, thriving community located on two major trade routes—the road from Thessalonica and the port at nearby Neapolis. She knew exactly what her customers wanted, and she was confident she provided the highest quality fabrics. Her suppliers in Thyatira had perfected the process of obtaining the dye from the spiny-shelled mollusk known as a murex.[4] She looked forward each day to engaging in commerce in this strategic area of the world. And she was rewarded for her efforts. Lydia was very wealthy and had a home with servants there in Philippi.

But money was not enough for Lydia. She noticed a restlessness early on, a hunger that all her possessions could not satisfy. She learned about some Jewish women meeting for prayer on the Sabbath at the river Gangitis, just west of Philippi. She was interested. She believed in God and longed to worship Him. *I'm not sure I'm ready to convert to Judaism, but I'm interested,* she thought to herself. So Lydia was known as a God-fearer; a Gentile who was deeply impressed by God yet unwilling to take the final steps to convert to Judaism. On the Sabbath, she made it a habit to join other Jewish women in prayer there at the riverside.

This day in particular felt special. Her hunger for God was deeper, stronger than usual. She longed for something more. She thought, *How can I feel such emptiness, such desire, when I seemingly have everything?* It was then she realized, *The substance of life is not contained in possessions or money. It can't be, or it would satisfy me. I would be fulfilled.* This eye-opening realization caused her to stop for a moment on this Sabbath day. She looked up at the sky, wondering about her Creator. *Who is He really? What is He like?* She smiled. *Lydia, for someone who is usually all business, you are thinking more deeply than usual about the meaning of life.* She looked down the road toward the riverside. She could already see some of the women there. She recognized some of the Jewish women who had been there in the past. She envied their heritage. They knew God better than she ever could, for they were born to know Him. She was on the outside looking in. Could she ever realize a fulfillment of her deepest heart's desire?

But what is this? Who are these strangers? She noticed they were walking up to the small band of women just as she arrived. They introduced themselves. Just imagine that first meeting!

"I'm Luke," said one. Then another, who seemed to be in charge, said, "I'm Paul. And God has sent us to you with a message." Lydia turned and looked at Paul. She definitely was interested in a message from God. He explained that they were trying to give their message in many parts of Asia but were forbidden by God, apparently for one main reason. God clearly showed them hungry hearts in Macedonia, including Philippi, who needed to hear their good news and receive their help.

Could it be? Only God could see her hungry heart. Had God sent these men in answer to a cry in her own heart? She shook her head, refusing to believe such a personal response was possible. But now Lydia was clearly listening, hanging on every word. She wondered what they were going to say.

The men sat down and began sharing words that filled her hungry heart like bread from heaven. They talked about sin and its corresponding penalty of death. Then they introduced everyone to a person, unseen yet very present: Jesus Christ. They spoke about His life, death, burial, and resurrection.

Drinking in every word, Lydia sensed a presence and an understanding she had not known before. She felt her heart open up to all that Paul was sharing. It was not a physical feeling, but a firm knowing, a new understanding of spiritual reality. She knew that what Paul was saying was true, and she felt as though she was given a gift, receiving a belief in his words about Christ. At some point she must have voiced her commitment: "I believe what you are saying is true. I want this new life you are talking about. I want to follow Christ and know God." She was so excited that she brought those in her household to hear, and because of her influence, they also believed.

Paul and those with him led her and her household into the river and baptized all of them, signifying the old life was gone and new life had begun. Now Lydia knew why she had felt a resistance to converting to Judaism. She saw it so clearly now. Jesus is the only way to God, for He paid the penalty for her sins and gave her new life. *I'm forgiven. Set free. Free to love and serve God.* She sensed this day marked the beginning of something new that would change everything about her. But she wanted to learn more. And she was eager to serve God in some way, to honor Christ with her life.

She said to Paul, Luke, and the others, "If you have judged me to be faithful to the Lord, come into my house and stay."

And thus began the ministry of Jesus Christ in Macedonia through the life of a wealthy woman who became rich in the Lord. Lydia became the first convert in Europe and opened the way for many others to hear about Christ. Her commitment was obviously a costly one, for

Paul and Silas ended up in the Philippian jail. Lydia was bold and courageous, and God used her in a mighty way. Her house became a meeting place for Christians, and her hospitality ministered to Paul, Luke, and other disciples (Acts 16:40).

Grace finds people who are poor in spirit and pours out spiritual riches on them. It is never easy for those with wealth and possessions to hold what they have with open hands in order to receive Christ. Jesus, with His keen ability to touch the heart of one's need, told a rich man to sell everything he had in order to follow Him. Jesus alone knew that this man's riches had a death-grip on his heart. But whether you are rich or poor, God's grace finds hungry hearts and offers them wealth in Christ. That Sabbath day, by the riverside, a wealthy woman in Philippi, hungry for God, became rich in Christ. Laying up her treasure in heaven, she influenced others to give their lives to Him.

✳

When we receive the gracious gift of all of our wealth in Christ, we live in the promise of abundant provision by God. He promises to provide for our needs whether we are rich or poor in this world (Philippians 4:19). The corresponding gift of grace for those who are rich in Christ is contentment (Philippians 4:11). Contentment is independent of outward circumstances and rests in the knowledge that what we have in Christ is enough. Contentment in Christ is learned and thus an aspect of our spiritual maturity as we walk with the Lord in the garden of grace. We learn contentment in the heat of adverse circumstances as we suffer while drawing on our spiritual wealth in Christ through the promises of God and the power of the Holy Spirit.

Contentment in Christ allows us to flourish in our current circumstances, assured the Lord desires to accomplish something in and through us right where we are. Walking closely with Him in the garden of grace, we listen for His guidance and direction so we can move in sync with Him wherever He has us. Our relationship with Christ is like a dance in which we lean into His embrace and follow His lead. In some cases, He may guide us to move in a new direction, as He did in the life of Mary Crowley. Sometimes He may choose to keep us right where we are, as He has during certain periods of my life. Sometimes the most difficult challenge for me has been enduring a season of waiting when even money for a meal requires trust in God's promises. My mother shares that some of her most amazing moments were the times when there was no food on the table to feed my brother and me. And then she would receive a phone call from the church—at just the right time—offering a job to play the organ for a wedding.

Sometimes God will surprise you with something that will remind you that you are His princess and that you have an inheritance waiting for you in heaven. He gives you a magnanimous, over-the-top gift of His grace. I think about the time many years ago when I moved to Julian to become Josh McDowell's personal secretary. Julian is a small town in Southern California, about an hour and a half's drive northeast of San Diego. Where would I live? Through the help of some friends, an opportunity opened up for me to live in a house owned by a San Diego family. Well, I wish you could have seen the house. It was a multilevel home with thousands of square feet of living area—a dream come true for me. Located out in the country, this magnificent home was situated next to wide-open land with pine trees everywhere. I used to sit in the living room and watch deer walk by the front window, or I'd sit outside and watch cows grazing in the pasture. Often, in my quiet time, looking at my multimillion-dollar view with tears in my eyes, I would say, *Lord, thank You for Your gift to me. I could have never orchestrated such a place to live. You sure take good care of me.* Although I was quite poor, I lived like a queen!

I often remember God's provision of that house in my journeys into the land of contentment, where I am learning to rest in Christ, realizing He is my sufficiency and enough for me. And how does the Lord help us understand our riches in Him and become more contented in Him? Sometimes He will ask us to lay aside our rights to some material possessions. We may experience the loss of a profession or a dream home or some such thing. If the Lord asks you to lay down your rights to some material thing that you love, take heart. Whatever the material item, if it is temporal, it will not last forever anyway.

I remember my last day in my dream home, just before closing the door on that chapter in my life. As I looked out the window, the Lord gave me a new thought. I realized, *Catherine, even if you lived in this house until your dying day, you would still have to say goodbye to it when you step from time into eternity. So why not say goodbye now?* What an incredible peace and contentment the Lord gave me in that moment. I grew spiritually deeper in my relationship with Christ that day. My eternal riches in Him mean so much more to me now.

Ponnamal experienced a moment when she had to lay aside her rights to something very precious to her—her jewelry. According to custom and tradition in India, a woman's jewelry was very important to her. While Ponnamal was preaching, she heard a child say to her mother, "I would like to join the group and wear jewels like that sister." Ponnamal felt her face flush with embarrassment on hearing those words.

Convicted by God, she resolved to remove her jewels. And God gave her the promise, "You also will be a crown of beauty in the hand of the LORD, and a royal diadem in the hand of your God" (Isaiah 62:3). Though she would be unjewelled in the eyes of others, she was not to her Lord. When she arrived home, she took off her jewels, realizing she possessed so much more in Christ. Soon, others in their groups removed their jewels as well, serving as an example for all who heard their message. And ultimately, their group traveled with less danger, as their jewels did not lure robbers to steal from them.

If God asks you to set something aside for the sake of the gospel, you can be sure He has good reasons. I surely know the wrestling in my own heart at times when I need to lay something down. But I know my God can be trusted. Often you will learn the reasons why only after days or even years have passed. And if you never learn the reason this side of heaven, someday when you are face-to-face with God, you will see the beauty of His plan.

Do you struggle with contentment? I understand, for I also struggle at times. But I am learning not to fear any need in my life, for I already have everything in Christ. He is always more than any material possession, and He is enough. Even though I wrestle with some losses, ultimately God, by His grace, in the power of His Spirit, enables me to let go and trust in Him. When you believe in Him and receive your wealth in Him, you will travel far on the pathway of spiritual growth, experiencing a new walk in grace.

Part 3

The Growth in Grace

SEASONS OF THE SOUL

She looked out the window and saw the U.S. Marine Corps car pull up in front of her house. Her heart sank. Barbara braced herself, already sensing the news. She had heard bad news before. She remembered the day when she received the call about her husband's near-fatal automobile accident. But God had miraculously healed and restored her precious husband, Bill, to her. But she knew this news would be life-altering. And her worst fears were confirmed with the officer's words. Her handsome 18-year-old son had died near Da Nang in the Vietnam War. *He is safe in the arms of Jesus now. No more suffering,* she thought.

Stick a Geranium in Your Hat and Be Happy is the title of one of Barbara Johnson's early books. How could anyone who had suffered so much say such seemingly flippant words? Barbara endured the deepest, most painful seasons of the soul, and she also personally experienced the sufficiency of God's grace in the heat of the fiery trial. After her son's death in Vietnam, another son was killed by a drunk driver. Then she and her husband were estranged from another son for 11 years while he struggled with a lifestyle of homosexuality.

When asked about her positive attitude in spite of all she's been through, this is how Barbara responded:

God has fine-tuned me. I lost my dad when I was twelve, then I lost one son and then the next son. So I've been through a lot of losses. One son was lost in Vietnam and one killed by a drunk driver. I think because I have been through that and I have experienced a lot of pain that I have credentials. They *have* to listen to me. I'm not just being funny, telling jokes. I have been in the pits. I have been where I wanted to die, where I wanted to kill myself and to kill anyone else [she laughs]. I've come through it, and God has infused me with a lot of joy. That's what I want to use, to get into my books as I share my books with people so they can use it and be a conduit of God's love too.

Barbara drew near to God, listened to Him, and responded with grace. Then she witnessed firsthand His touch of grace, taking her to a new place in her relationship with Him. Each fiery trial led to a new avenue of ministry. When her son was killed in Vietnam, she shared God's grace with other parents who had also lost sons in the war. With her second son's death, she gained an eternal perspective about real life face-to-face with God in heaven. She and her husband held a coronation service, celebrating their son's new life with the Lord in heaven. Through this time, she saw many others touched as a result.

Her other son's gay lifestyle seemed more difficult to process. She couldn't escape the reality of his choices. But she determined in her heart to survive this season with triumph and victory, drawing once again on the grace of God. She and her husband responded to God's leading and founded Spatula Ministries in 1978 to "scrape people off the ceiling, which is where they land when they discover a child, husband, or wife is having a homosexual or lesbian relationship."

Oh, how we need at least a thousand more Barbara Johnsons in this world! She communicated to the world what became known as her trademark "outrageous joy." God opened the door for her to share her words of hope with thousands of women at the Women of Faith conferences.

> There is universal pain. God can take your trouble and change it into treasure. Your sorrow can be exchanged for joy, not just a momentary smile, but a deep new joy…Give God the pain and sorrow; give Him the guilt you feel. Tears and heartaches come to us all. They are part of living, but Jesus Christ can ease the heartache.

Barbara's words offer hope because she has walked the road of pain through the deepest, darkest seasons of life. In 2001 she was diagnosed with a brain tumor and valiantly battled central nervous system lymphoma for six years. She continued writing and joked in those years that each book was called her last book. She said she had at least six last books.

> I decided since I wasn't moving on to perpetual retirement, I might as well get back to work…Frankly, it's a little embarrassing, after all these enthusiastic farewells, to still be down here gathering goofy stuff when I thought I'd be singing with the saints by now. But here it is 2007, and I'm still living, still laughing, and still growing older…I don't know about you, but I now plan to live happily to be one hundred—or die trying!

Those grace-filled words were so "Barbara"—she breathed out the grace of God whenever she wrote or spoke.

Barbara Johnson stepped from time into eternity with her Lord in 2007, but her hope and joy borne through the seasons of life and won in the soul through God's grace live on in her books.

> God makes gold out of our lives one way or another—in the furnace of pain and suffering or in some manner of waiting. But while we are "in the furnace," it is important to understand we are there for a reason and that nothing comes into our lives but through God's filter. Whatever he sends, he gives grace enough for us to carry through.[1]

✳

God's grace is enough for every season of the soul. We do travel through seasons, no doubt about it. I view my own life as a pilgrimage of the heart through seasons of the soul. Solomon said in Ecclesiastes 3:1 (NIV), "There is a time for everything, and a season for every activity under heaven." When we walk in the garden of grace, Jesus gives us what we need in every season of the soul. Through the seasons, God makes a saint. We grow spiritually through the seasons because His grace is enough to revive, restore, and renew us. That's why the garden of grace is the perfect environment for growth. Sometimes the seasons with the most pain bring the most growth. The crises we experience in some seasons lead to spiritual breakthroughs, resulting in new growth. Growth is a process in which God makes us trophies of His grace, giving a message of hope to the world.

Barbara Johnson is a perfect example of one who understood the seasons of the soul and relied on God to help her make it through. She used to say that we are pilgrims, not settlers. Life on earth does not last forever, and there will come a day when we step from time into eternity. During our brief stay on earth, understanding some of the seasons of our soul will help us hang in there, knowing God's grace will carry us through.

Just think about God's creative hand in the various seasons on earth. My mother has a pitcher filled with vibrant red, yellow, and orange-colored leaves gathered from the ground on a crisp fall day in Pennsylvania. I remember winters on the east coast when the bright white snow fell softly on the ground, blanketing the surroundings and transforming them into a winter wonderland. And what about spring, with birds chirping and flowers blooming in well-tended gardens? I loved summers growing up because they brought freedom to play, go on picnics, and read books without interruption. Each season is so special in its own beautiful and unique way.

In the same way, God takes us through seasons in our souls, each one unique and personal. God does a mighty work in each season, making us His masterpiece (Ephesians 2:10) and using us for His glory. Chuck Swindoll, in his book *Growing Strong in the Seasons of Life*, describes four distinct seasons: winter, a season of quiet reverence; spring, a season of refreshing renewal; summer, a season of rest; and autumn, a season of nostalgic reflection.[2] He said, "Our hope is to grow stronger and taller as our roots dig deeper in the soft soil along the banks of the river of life." I love those words, for they describe our growth in the grace of the Lord through the seasons of life.

I believe there are many seasons of the soul for us, and God carries us through each one. You and I need God's grace to make it through the seasons of the soul. His grace gives us His magnificent promises for every season, enabling us to endure and hope in Him.

Years ago, I looked into the eyes of a pastor who was defeated and discouraged. Life had become tough for him in his place of ministry, and he had given up. Now he was working in a store and trying to forget his call to ministry. Short on money and disillusioned, he was selling his library of Bible reference books.

Perhaps God was leading him in a new direction. But surveys reveal that 50 percent of pastors are so discouraged, they would leave the ministry if they could. I wonder if some in the ministry give up because they forget the seasons in life won't last forever and that God will hold them close to His heart in trials. And God offers His promises to give us hope, especially in the darkest seasons of our lives.

We need the Word of God to tether our hearts to Him so we don't give up in the most difficult seasons of life. We draw on God's grace every moment, receiving what we need so we can hang on and stand strong. And then, in His grace, we grow. We become the women He wants us to be.

What are some of the seasons of the soul we will journey through as we walk with the Lord in the garden of grace? There are many, but here are some of the most common seasons.

The season of tears. I mention this season first because I think I have known it the most in my own life. And Barbara Johnson surely did as well. Psalm 84:6 names this soul season the "valley of weeping." This is when you are broken, perhaps even devastated and tempted to fall into despair. You are experiencing some kind of loss. It may be a loss of a loved one, physical health, a job, a home, or your security. Some of the greatest growth occurs in the season of tears, for it rocks your boat, awakening sensitivities in your soul you may not have even known were there. Though you may be hurting deeply, you can experience God's presence in ways other people cannot possibly know. By God's grace, He gives blessed treasure in your darkness (Isaiah 45:3) and enables you to trust Him in the trial.

The season of joy. Sometimes this exuberant, exciting season occurs just after a season of tears. In fact, the psalmist said that real pilgrims whose strength is in the Lord enjoy blessings in the midst of the valley of weeping. Most of the time the season of joy is unexpected, arriving at the harbor of your soul as God's surprise. God seems to delight in surprising His saints with fresh touches of His love, resulting in a deep joy.

Joy is independent of circumstances and rests on the activity and presence of God in your life. Regardless of whether the floodwaters of life recede, joy is possible because of Christ in you. Nehemiah tells us that the joy of the Lord is our strength (Nehemiah 8:10). When Jesus spoke with His disciples, He pointed out that His purpose was to give them His joy (John 15:11). When you need a fresh dose of joy, open the pages of God's Word and allow the words of Jesus to penetrate your heart. Cultivate an expectation that joy will rain on your heart, for God promises that joy will come in the morning (Psalm 30:5). God's grace will help you cultivate a heart of gratitude and thankfulness for His manifold blessings.

The season of wrestling. In this season, you are struggling to understand what God is doing in your life. You may feel disillusioned with God, but you are coming to grips with His ways and are realizing they are higher than your ways (Isaiah 55:8-9). God is bringing you to a place where you yield to His ways in your life. And in fact, this bend in the road, which seems such a stumbling block to you, is most likely leading you to a new, broad place of life and ministry. But the very fact that you cannot see the result is causing you to wrestle. This wrestling can eventually lead to a new and stronger faith in God and His Word. God's grace helps you give way to His ways and trust in Him rather than relying on your own understanding (Proverbs 3:5-6).

The season of productivity. God has created you for a purpose and has prepared good works for you (Ephesians 2:10). This season may include caring for your family, serving in a ministry, or working in a profession or job. In the season of productivity, you're just plain busy and producing a lot. A time of productivity means hard work and fatigue. But you can know that your toil is not in vain when accomplished in the power of the Lord (1 Corinthians 15:58). And you need God's power for these times of great responsibility, for there will be moments when you think you cannot make it one more step. God's grace will help you rely on God for strength to serve Him well in all your work.

The season of weakness. In the season of weakness, you may suffer from an illness, a disability, or overwhelming exhaustion. In this season, you become aware that you are not enough in your own strength. You can never carry out God's assignments in your own strength. This may be obvious to some, but sometimes we feel as though we can do anything God asks of us. Great is the moment when you become aware of your own inability, failure, or frailty. Why? You will turn away from yourself and run to God for His inexhaustible supply of strength.

The apostle Paul knew this season when he experienced a thorn in the flesh that left him depleted and devastated. He begged God to remove the thorn so he could successfully serve Him. In this season, we are misinformed, thinking we could run our race if only we could have what we want or get rid of what we don't want in our lives. What God wants us to know is that we are *in the race.* We don't need to have or get rid of anything to run our race. God is enough. In Paul's case, God said, "My grace is sufficient for you" (2 Corinthians 12:9). Paul discovered the sufficiency of God, realizing that his weakness made him strong. God's grace in the season of weakness enables you to draw on His strength and power, making you more than you could ever be on your own.

The season of repentance. In this season you become aware of your sin, and you are brokenhearted at your failure. You fall on your face before God and say, *I'm sorry, Lord.* You agree with God about your sin. More than anything, you wish you could start over. Then you realize in a new way the power of the cross. You're forgiven. However deeply you may have fallen into sin, His love and forgiveness are deeper still. You may experience weeping because you are so devastated at your failure. But you need to realize in this season that you have "great feet of clay." You live in an earthen vessel. You tend toward sin, but thankfully, you are no longer a slave to sin. You can say yes to God and no to sin. John tells us in his epistle that if we say we have no sin, we make God a liar. But he continues by saying that if we confess our sins, He forgives us (1 John 1:9). God's grace will help you confess your sin in these times and be filled with His Spirit.

The season of waiting. In this season, you hold on to God's promises, yet He seems to say, *Wait for Me; it's not time yet.* You are like David, who prayed to God and eagerly watched to see what God was going to do (Psalm 5:3). Times of waiting are biblical. Hannah prayed and waited for a child for many years before Samuel was born. David waited for years before God fulfilled His promise to make him king.

In the season of waiting, you hope in God's Word, and you wait for the Lord (Psalm 130:5-6). In the season of waiting, you trust in God's timing and in His purpose. God's grace helps you wait with the hope that God will give you exactly what you need, though not necessarily what you want.

The season of endurance. This season is similar to the season of waiting except that often you are experiencing hardship or bearing pain. The hand of God is pressing heavily on you, and you need a supernatural ability to bear things, not with resignation, but with a blazing hope. In this season the trial is prolonged, and you are feeling like David must have felt when he said, "How long, O LORD? Will you forget me forever?" (Psalm 13:1). In the times of endurance, you may feel as though you cannot make it one more minute. You need to know that God never forgets you and is working out His purpose. The promises of God will carry you through the season of endurance. God's grace empowers you to draw upon the promises of God and walk with Him by faith.

The season of reflection. God encourages His people, "Be still and know that I am God" (Psalm 46:10). Our hearts and souls require reflection to flourish. As you walk with God in the garden of grace, don't be surprised if you sometimes feel as though you are set on a shelf in virtual obscurity. God is giving you a season of reflection. Take advantage of it, for these times don't usually last very long. God sometimes guides us to intentionally choose to enter a season of reflection. Occasionally you need to slow down to focus on God and think deep thoughts. You will be amazed how these times of reflection lead to times of refreshing, for you will experience God's presence (Acts 3:19). God's grace gives you the ability to respond to His call for reflection and slow down, creating more space for Him.

The season of rest. This season is like a spa for the soul. Jesus takes you into this season when He says, "Come away with me by yourselves and rest a little while" (Mark 6:31 WILLIAMS). In your time of rest you may go undercover, so to speak, and step away from ministry responsibilities. Most women feel guilty taking time to rest, but you need a rest. Your heart and soul require it, and you will be amazed how rejuvenated you are after you experience this season. God's grace enables you to step away from certain responsibilities for a while.

You may recognize yourself in all the seasons, for they represent experiences you have had in your own pilgrimage with the Lord. God's purpose is woven through all the seasons of the soul. Each season is so very valuable in your walk with God in the garden of grace. Spiritual growth is definitely a process. God promises He has begun a good work in you, He will perfect it until the day of Christ, and He is accomplishing His will in and through you. Not only that, His progressive work in you brings Him pleasure. Do you know what this means for you? Spiritual growth through the seasons of the soul is a winning proposition. God can't fail. Even though you may feel weak and helpless, especially in the midst of some of the most painful seasons, you can take courage in God's gift of unfailing love and purpose.

✳

She did not ask for this humiliation. In fact, sometimes Abigail wondered how someone as smart as she was could be in such a situation. She was trapped, or so she felt. Everyone had thought she was privileged to marry Nabal. He was rich, owned livestock, and had business dealing in other villages. But she had not known he was harsh and mean. Once married, she had experienced his evil side. He lashed out at her almost every day. She did not deserve such treatment. As beautiful as she was, any man would have enjoyed her as his wife. But Nabal was not like other men. He did not appreciate anything he had and always expected more. He was dissatisfied with everyone and everything.

Abigail had learned every nuance of his character through the years. She knew how to deal with him, for she was wise. There was no reasoning with him in those moments when his temper flew out of control. Those were the times when he bordered on insanity. Through this terrible, horrible season of her life, she cast herself on the Lord, entrusting her soul to Him. She resolved to do what was right and true in God's eyes and set out to please Him. And she came to a few conclusions about her husband. He could never be pleased with her in his current spiritual condition. He was a fool. He was arrogant, consumed with himself, and did not respect God.

Abigail had heard about David, his defeat of the giant Goliath, and his love for God. She knew that he and his 600 men had protected her husband's flocks, allowing him to prosper. It was shearing season, and

Nabal was out in the field shearing his sheep. And Abigail was about to experience a turn of events that would change her life forever.

David sent ten of his men to Nabal with a message. "Greet him in my name…have a long life, peace to you…peace be to all that you have." But David also sent a request to Nabal, "Please give whatever you find at hand to your servants and to your son David" (1 Samuel 25:5-6,8). David was in need of provisions and thought Nabal would be more than willing to help him out in light of the gracious protection he was receiving. David had not counted on Nabal's wickedness.

Nabal responded, "Who is David? And who is the son of Jesse?" He continued on, telling David that he could care less who he was and had no intention of giving him anything. Nabal was not remotely aware of his recklessness in rejecting David, thus proving the greatness of his folly.

"What is it?" asked Abigail. One of the young men had stormed in and called out her name. He was panicked. "David sent messengers from the wilderness to greet our master, and he scorned them."

Abigail's heart felt as though it would melt. Horrified at the stupidity of her husband, she resolved to somehow make amends. Her only hope was to intervene and beg for mercy, counting on David's famous kindness and mercy. She ordered her servants to go ahead of her. She knew what she would do. She could make her way around the other side of the mountain and meet David without her husband ever knowing. She loaded food on one donkey and rode her own donkey, praying they would meet David before he killed her husband and his men. She could not even imagine how insulted David must feel. She knew how her husband had humiliated her. And at times, the desire to retaliate was almost more than she could bear. But God gave her patience and strength to endure Nabal's foolish oppression.

She saw David in the distance. With pounding heart, she dismounted and ran toward him. Falling on her face, she bowed at his feet, and said, "On me alone, my lord, be the blame. And please let your maidservant speak to you, and listen to the words of your maidservant. Please do not let my lord pay attention to this worthless man, Nabal…" She continued to describe Nabal in candid language because she knew him almost better than she knew herself. She appealed to David, asking forgiveness and reminded him not to avenge himself, but to leave vengeance to the Lord. Then she wisely presented David with God's promise: "The lives of your enemies He will sling out…And when the Lord does for my lord according to all the good that He has spoken concerning you, and appoints you ruler over Israel, this will not cause grief or a troubled heart to my lord." And finally, as if an afterthought, she asked the man who would someday be king, "When the Lord deals well with my lord, then remember your maidservant" (1 Samuel 25:29-31).

She watched David, unsure how he would respond. But she knew he was a good man, highly favored by God. He was so different from Nabal, her own husband. She heard David respond with words she had never heard from Nabal: "Blessed be the Lord God of Israel, who sent you this day to meet me, and blessed be your discernment, and blessed be you…" David told her to go in peace and that he heard her and granted her request.

Abigail practically flew home. She felt so blessed. She wondered how she would tell Nabal that his life had been spared. Exuberant, she entered the house. Quickly her joy turned to shock. Her husband was holding a feast, gloating at his supposed victory over David and imagining himself to be king of his own domain. She had seen him like this before but never quite so drunk. She quietly slipped into the bedroom, crawled under the covers, and waited, shaking, wondering what the new day would bring.

She found Nabal the next morning slouched over but finally sober after a long night. She told him that his life had been spared by David. She could see that for the first time, perhaps, he grasped the enormity of his own foolish action. The days moved in fast-forward for Abigail after she spoke with Nabal. Having heard the news from Abigail, Nabal's heart failed, and he was dead ten days later. How quickly seasons in a life could change. When David heard the news about Nabal's death, he sent his servants to say to Abigail, "David has sent us to you to take you as his wife." And so Abigail's season of tears was turned to a season of joy that day, and she became the wife of David, the man after God's own heart and God's chosen king.

✳

How quickly seasons of the soul can change in our lives. The one constant is God Himself, who pours His grace into our hearts to help us respond to Him and experience personal revival as we walk with Him. We need to believe God in every season and receive His gifts of grace as He provides us with whatever we need.

Being aware of the season I am in helps me make it through. I realize that this too shall pass. Then I am able to recognize my need and look for promises in God's Word for hope and encouragement. One friend recently told me about the change of seasons in her life:

> Right now, my oldest daughter has graduated high school and is excited about the next step in her life. My wonderful 16-year-old son is faced with choices in sports that are really tearing him apart. Last night, I was sitting in church and musing about this new chapter in my life—that of parenting teenagers and having a young adult. The challenge for me is to continue to encourage my babies to seek God first, to consider Him in all things, to realize that the next step in our lives is His doing.

Another friend is currently in a season of tears and endurance, helping her husband through a difficult rehabilitation after a devastating stroke that caught them both by surprise.

What season of the soul are you traveling through in your own pilgrimage? You can know that no season, whatever it may be, is a surprise to your Lord. In fact, He is walking with you in this garden of grace through all your seasons, and He will be your constant companion, giving joy in the journey. Believe it, receive it, and live it.

9

THE DOOR IS ALWAYS OPEN

"Working with women in your own church, would you be able to discover in a six-month period what happens when women pray?" Evelyn Christenson could not forget that question. In fact, the more she thought about it, the more she prayed. Finally, she was compelled to begin a prayer experiment. What would God do when women pray? Only a few women joined in her experiment at first. The results were astounding as people became Christians and lives were transformed.

A long-distance call came to their church one Sunday after the morning service. A man, Arthur Blessitt, asked, "May I use the church building to hold an evangelistic meeting for young people?" In those days, the young people he wanted to reach were called hippies. He just wanted to reach hippies for Christ. Evelyn's husband responded, "Fine. You may use our church."

Arthur arrived on Tuesday morning, the same time Evelyn met with her women for prayer. The turnout for the evangelistic meeting that night did not look too promising because the only advertising had been by word of mouth. So Evelyn and her group fervently prayed for God to make something happen to turn the tide and reach young people in their city for Christ.

As they were praying, Carolyn, the church secretary interrupted

151

them. "The religion editor of the newspaper came to interview Arthur Blessitt; now they're on their knees praying!" The religion editor received Christ and ran a front-page story about the evangelistic meeting at the church in the afternoon edition. More than 1100 attended that evening. Some had come as far as 90 miles. Many were trapped in sin, some even using hard drugs. When Arthur gave the invitation, more than 100 young people came to Christ. People were praying everywhere—in hallways, corridors, and meeting rooms—and the presence of God was evident in that place.

Evelyn discovered that storming the throne room of heaven with prayer really did make a difference. She was astounded with the results. In fact, her conviction to pray deepened, and she was filled with a desire to encourage others to develop a life of prayer. She decided to write *What Happens When Women Pray*, a book about the results of her simple experiment of prayer.

The book Evelyn wrote sold two million copies, impacting the prayer lives of women worldwide. Her words on prayer encourage others to boldly enter the throne room of God and present their requests to Him. Evelyn shows that courageous prayer makes a difference with God. She founded United Prayer Ministry when she read Revelation 3:8: "Behold, I have put before you an open door." She received those words as God's assignment for her to teach on prayer, write about prayer, and encourage others to a deep commitment to prayer. She describes her prayer ministry as "ordinary women doing not so ordinary things by the grace of God through prayer."

Evelyn relies on prayer for every aspect of her life and ministry. And she loves praying with others, believing the real power comes when we enter the throne room of God with groups of people. She describes her practice:

> Since 1964, I have not even taught a Sunday school class without someone praying for me. I have not ventured overseas unless the 1000-member 24-hour prayer clock was

activated—each intercessor taking a segment of the day or night. I have never written a book, traveled to a seminar or run a committee meeting without my prayer board praying for me on a daily basis through using a telephone prayer chain, and praying *with* me on a monthly basis. Like Joshua, I have experienced awesome results from my solitary prayers; but I have also found the added comfort, support and love of those who have faithfully and persistently prayed with me. These prayers have held up my hands, like Moses' two friends held up his (see Exodus 17:12).

Evelyn learned from God the need to pray with purpose, drawing near to the throne of gace. She is most burdened about the urgent need for prayer warriors, explaining, "When we are convicted by the idea that those without Jesus are lost eternally—whether it's a child rebelling and rejecting God, a struggling family member who won't accept Him, or a person who's never heard of him—this is when we bombard heaven unceasingly."

Do you share Evelyn's burden for prayer? If not, don't worry. If you are walking with God in the garden of grace, you will become a woman of prayer. You can't stop your life of prayer from growing when you walk with Jesus. Grace draws you into conversation with God. When you receive gift after gift from God, all undeserved, you are pulled like a magnet to God. He becomes central in your life. And the more you know His grace, the more you realize His absolute delight in answering your prayers.

✳

He assumed his familiar position by the road out of Jericho. Perhaps today he would receive a few coins from a merciful traveler leaving the city. Blind and poor, Bartimaeus was relegated to begging by the side of a road. What a hopeless piece of existence he had. His position in life had revealed to him the true nature of man. There was no mercy for one like him. People mostly lived by the motto "Me first and no rules." Actions spoke more loudly than words. Very few even noticed him sitting there. He blended into the background, invisible to the world. More than anything he wished he could see. Why did he have no sight? He couldn't even begin to understand the answer to that deep, painful question.

But recently, a kernel of hope had sprouted in his soul. He could not explain the thoughts bombarding his mind when he heard about Jesus the Nazarene. He learned that people were healed of diseases; a paralyzed man had walked, and a girl had been raised from the dead. If Jesus healed them, maybe He could make a blind man see. He shook his head just thinking about such a possibility. Then he laughed. Could he even hope for such a miracle? But the eyewitness accounts of healing were undisputed. His thoughts went wild as he considered what might happen if he could find Jesus.

Time seemed to blend together for Bartimaeus. Hours melded together to form endless days. But today Bartimaeus could feel an excitement in the atmosphere of Jericho. And in the distance he could hear many voices. He could feel the movement in the ground. A crowd of people was making its way toward him. *What's going on in Jericho?* Then he heard voices. "Jesus is coming this way. It's Jesus the Nazarene."

"Jesus, Son of David, have mercy on me!" The words rose up from deep within, before he could think of stopping himself. He knew what he wanted. And Jesus was his only hope. "Jesus, Son of David, have mercy on me!" he desperately cried.

Voices in the crowd sternly admonished Bartimaeus to be quiet. But Bartimaeus cried out all the more, "Jesus, Son of David, have mercy on me!"

Then the unthinkable became reality. Jesus stopped and said, "Call him here."

Bartimaeus never heard His words. He only knew the music of the unnamed voices who came and said, "Take courage, stand up! He is calling for you."

Without hesitation, throwing off his cloak, Bartimaeus jumped up and followed others to Jesus.

Then Bartimaeus heard the most beautiful voice with words he would remember for the rest of his life. "What do you want Me to do for you?" (Luke 18:41). Bartimaeus felt as though Jesus was continuing a conversation that had begun with his own cry for mercy. He realized in an instant that Jesus had heard and entered into his plea before he even made it.

"Rabboni, I want to regain my sight!" Bartimaeus knew his deepest desire.

Jesus said to him, "Go; your faith has made you well."

There was no passage of time between the words and the action. Immediately, Jesus spoke, and Bartimaeus could see. His first view was most beautiful, looking into the face and eyes of the one who restored his sight.

What could Bartimaeus say in this defining moment? Jesus turned and kept walking down the road out of Jericho. His disciples gathered around Him. Bartimaeus knew no words were necessary. He looked back at his place by the side of the road and smiled. Never again would he assume the position of a beggar, for now he knew the King of kings. Now he would follow Jesus. He turned and started walking down the road, blending in with the crowd. No longer invisible, he was known by the one who knows every heart.

✳

I love reading about Bartimaeus's healing, for I believe it gives us a glimpse into God's gracious and merciful heart. I also believe this one event helps us understand prayer in a way that encourages us to enter into the great privilege afforded us as His children. When we truly understand God's willingness to hear and answer our prayers, we will pray.

The Gospel of Mark reveals that when Jesus spoke to Bartimaeus, He "answered" him (10:51). That one word means that Jesus heard his cry. Jesus entered into the conversation with Bartimaeus. And He answered with some of the most wonderful words anyone could possibly hear from God, the Creator of the universe, King of kings and Lord of lords. Imagine what it must have meant for Bartimaeus to hear Jesus respond to his cry by asking, "What do you want Me to do for you?" In this one question, Jesus is explaining the Father's heart of grace to us. He is asking you, "What do you want Me to do for you?" He is asking me, "What do you want Me to do for you?" When you think of prayer, imagine Jesus asking you the same question. He is waiting to pour out grace and mercy to meet your deepest needs.

God invites us, His children, into His throne room. And when we arrive, what do we find? According to the writer of Hebrews, we discover a throne of grace (Hebrews 4:16). And we are invited by God Himself to draw near with confidence. Because of grace, when we enter the throne room, we find the favor and smile of God. And there is one who understands our suffering, our need, our desire, and enters into our dilemma with us, whatever our circumstance may be. Jesus sympathizes with our weakness (Hebrews 4:15). Author Jerry Bridges explains that this means Jesus possesses the "capacity for sharing or understanding the feelings of another person. This feeling can be felt only by a person who has experienced the same or similar trials and who, consequently, understands what the other person is going through and has a desire to relieve the other's distress."[1]

We have a multitude of misconceptions about God when it comes to prayer. We think we must convince God. Or maybe we must pray enough times before He'll answer. Or possibly He just didn't hear because we didn't use the right words. Maybe He's just too busy. In the movie *Bruce Almighty,* Bruce Nolan (Jim Carrey) has lost his job and blames God for everything that happens in his life. He tells God that He doesn't know how to run things on earth. Bruce is given a chance to take over God's responsibilities for a while so he can catch a glimpse of God's perspective. He begins receiving prayer requests in the form of Post-it notes. Soon millions of Post-it notes fill his room and his house, overflowing into the yard.

Such a picture gives us the idea that God couldn't possibly hear our prayers. But we forget that God is God, and we are not. He is infinite and eternal, and He can handle the impossible. He is Creator, *Elohim,* the one true God, who is able to create something out of nothing, count the stars, and number each hair on your head. We need to understand and count on God's promise to hear and answer our prayers.

God is telling us to never hesitate to storm the throne of grace and draw near to Him. The door is always open. Don't stand at a distance, but go right in and tell Him what you want. Our bold prayer is the means of appropriating and taking possession of all the gracious gifts that are ours in Jesus Christ. God's bountiful grace gives and gives and gives. He seems to be saying to us, "Just ask." No wonder James says, "You do not have because you do not ask" (James 4:2). Nineteenth-century preacher Phillips Brooks said, "Prayer is not conquering God's reluctance, but laying hold of God's willingness."

Drawing near to God in prayer enables us to receive by faith what we already have because of God's grace. An abundance of mercy is poured out on us from the throne of grace. Oh, the mercy of God! When I was a little girl, I rode my bicycle straight into a wall because I didn't know how to apply the brake. I took quite a fall and subsequently scraped my knee. Crying, I ran into the house and straight into my mother's arms. She cleaned me up and applied a soothing white cream. Instantly, I felt better. The mercy of God is His soothing balm of compassion, applied to the distresses of our heart.

When you pray, God makes things happen in your life. Evelyn Christenson points out that God does answer our prayers, but she adds, "It is the unexpected results we didn't even know to pray for that have kept us constantly praising God. The reason is not only because people pray but also because the omnipotent God of heaven hears and answers our prayers." God promises that you will "receive mercy and find grace to help in time of need" when you come to His throne of grace (Hebrews 4:16). And He just may surprise you with more than you had hoped.

Billy Graham was once asked what the secret was behind his evangelistic crusades. He replied, "There are three secrets. Prayer, prayer, and prayer."

Your bold approach to the throne of grace is contagious. Others are going to want to join you. One Michigan University student decided to form a dormitory house of prayer, committing to pray for fellow students each week. The response was so positive that seven more dorms committed to praying weekly for students. Lives were transformed, young people were becoming Christians, and soon every dormitory had a prayer group talking with God on a regular basis.

There are many ways to walk and talk with God when you draw near in prayer. Author Henri Nouwen describes a few:

> Sometimes we seek out a quiet spot and want to be alone, sometimes we look for a friend and want to be together. Sometimes we like a book, sometimes we prefer music. Sometimes we sing out with hundreds, sometimes only whisper with a few. Sometimes we want to say it with words, sometimes with a deep silence.[2]

Sometimes I like to write out my prayers in my *Quiet Time Notebook.* I love reading through my notebook later and remembering how God has answered my prayers. Other times I sit in my quiet place, close my eyes, and talk with God about all that is burdening my heart. I am learning to have an ongoing conversation with God, walking and talking with Him throughout the day. A person can pray on a mountain trail, with a husband at night, with a child before school, alone in quiet time, at a desk, in a prison cell, in a hospital, in an airplane... Wherever you are, you can pray, so always pray.

Psalms, the prayer book of the Bible, will help you draw near in prayer to the throne of grace. I have discovered that the psalmists were skilled in pouring out their hearts to the Lord. Jesus often quoted the psalms and sometimes used them in His prayers. When He spoke of the cross in John 12:27, He quoted from Psalm 6:3, "My soul is greatly dismayed…" When He was on the cross, He used the words of Psalm 22:1. If you find you do not know what to pray or even how to draw near to God, run to the psalms and pray the words, personalizing each phrase to communicate with Him.

Sometimes during the night I feel called by the Lord to pray, usually because of a burdened heart. In the darkness I make my way to our living room, where I fall on my knees and pour out my heart to the Lord at the throne of grace. These intimate times, usually lasting only ten or fifteen minutes, are precious prayer growth times for me. David meditated on the Lord in the night (Psalm 63:6), and the sons of Korah remembered the Lord's song in the night and prayed (Psalm 42:8).

I seem to sense the Lord's presence in the night in ways I can't when I'm in the busyness of my days. I've enjoyed these periodic night sessions with the Lord for about 30 years now and continue to look forward to His call in the night. The door leading to the throne of grace is always open, day or night. I just seem to sense that open door better at night, especially during my most difficult trials.

Will you get what you want when you pray? Not always, for God's grace can only give good and perfect gifts to His children. And sometimes, what we ask for is not what we really need. For we never see the full picture in panorama, from eternity past to eternity future, the way God does. We can't see hearts the way God can. And so, in our prayers, we pour out our hearts' desires and then trust in our Father's character of love, mercy, grace, and wisdom. Stand on God's promises that He gives every good and perfect gift and that He will not withhold any good thing from those who walk uprightly (James 1:17; Psalm 84:11).

Prayer is another magnificent gift in the garden of grace, for God is giving us open access to Himself (Ephesians 2:18). We have His ear at all times. I wonder if you have ever poured your heart out to loved ones, only to discover they were preoccupied with something else. They never even heard what you said. And how many times have people shared something meaningful with you, but you were distracted and missed their words? God always listens and hears every word. He is never distracted or preoccupied.

Brian Edwards' wife, Barbara, was recovering in the hospital after a serious spinal operation. She received an encouraging card from Violet, a 92-year-old member of their church. Violet closed the card with these words, "Cheer up. God is with you, for I have committed you in His care—and He is a very good listener. Goodnight. Wish you have a very good rest. And God bless you and keep you."[3] Violet understood the grace of God's listening ear. Brian, in his book *Grace—Amazing Grace,* points out that every time we pray, we express our consciousness of the privilege of being children of God, the delight of approaching Him, and "the certainty that he who is a good listener will hear us." He describes the magnificent grace of prayer this way: "Our God is awesomely powerful, blindingly holy, fearfully just and utterly other than us; but he is also a loving, caring Father to all his people, and he invites them to talk with him."[4]

Because God is "the God of all grace" (1 Peter 5:10), His door is always open for you. What do you need? Will you ask Him, even now? Don't waste one second in worry or fear when you can cry out to your Father in heaven.

✳

I received a call from my brother early one morning. I could tell from his voice that something was wrong.

"What's wrong, Rob? What's going on?"

"Cath, I got laid off. We just got the news that this is our last week."

"Oh Rob, I'm so sorry." Now the economic hardships hit close to home. My own brother had lost his job. I encouraged him for a few minutes and then felt tears welling up from deep inside. Rob and I are very close. We talk every day on the phone. And now I shared his devastation at being out of work. We discussed the positive aspects of this new occurrence in his life and possible opportunities for a new direction. After our call, I closed my eyes and prayed, *Lord, help my precious brother. Bring him a job that will be perfect for him. Lord, watch over his family and especially my little niece, Kayla. Lord, You know their needs better than I do. So help, Lord, help!* I pleaded with God to intervene and provide financially for Rob and his family.

But now, what would God do? At first, things went from bad to worse. Weeks went by until he received financial help from unemployment checks. My brother, highly knowledgeable in his field, was faced with every option any of us would have to consider to make a living. Would he have to work at minimum wage just to bring home some money in the interim until he found a higher-paying job? What about pursuing training for a career change? Just thinking through these decisions weighed heavily on my own heart as I shared my brother's burden. The weeks became months with no end in sight. My brother was becoming discouraged. With the jobless rate increasing nationwide, many other people saw him as simply another statistic. But he was not a number to me; he was my brother, whom I loved with all my heart.

One Monday, I was getting ready for work, and my thoughts turned to my brother. *My brother gets up, but he isn't getting ready for work, like me. Instead, he's wondering what he will be doing in the future. How will he provide for his family?* My heart felt increasingly burdened. In the moments that followed, I became passionate about prayer for Rob. I fell on my knees before the Lord, and prayed, *Lord, here is what I want. I'm laying this out before You, knowing You can do anything. Will you bring my brother the perfect job?* I spoke matter-of-factly with my Lord, imagining that I was personally handing my request to Him. I became much more serious about asking Him for help on behalf of my brother.

In fact, I could think of almost nothing else the entire week. Every free moment, I asked again. *Lord, what will You do on behalf of my brother?* I imagined Him asking me, *What do you want?* And I responded, *Lord, I want the perfect job for my brother. Please, Lord, help him in the way that only You can—miraculously, amazingly!*

On Friday afternoon, my mother called and said, "Catherine, has Rob called you yet?"

"No, Mother. What's going on?" I thought, *What now? Could it get any worse?*

"Catherine, I think Rob possibly has a job."

"What! Are you serious?"

"Yes, you'll have to talk to him. I don't know the details."

Well, of course I was excited. But I wasn't sure. Mother couldn't tell me about his job, so maybe she had misunderstood.

Strangely enough, I could not get in touch with my brother on Friday. But the next morning, he called. Our cell phones had a bad connection, and I could barely hear him. But he was excited. "Cath, I have a job! And it's going to be something new, in my field. I'll be able to use my expertise and have an office of my own."

Just as I was ready to respond, we got disconnected. I tried to call back, but no answer. Again, I fell on my knees and cried out, *Thank You, Lord, for answering our prayers.* Indeed, later I discovered that he had gotten a job that would capitalize on his knowledge and experience of 30 years. Only God could have orchestrated such an amazing answer to prayer.

But a new question arose for me. How was I to understand my experience of praying for three months? Were my previous prayers no good? Was it only when I became desperate that my prayers had meaning? I don't pretend to be an expert on prayer. But I do know that God encourages us to never give up in our prayers (Luke 18:1).

God's plans include timing issues that we just do not understand. We can't comprehend every detail because we are not God. And so, in prayer, I am learning to "press through" the circumstance, enter the throne room, and stay near the throne of grace, waiting on God for His answer. We need to draw on His grace to receive grace. I believe His grace helps us persevere in prayer. So in your circumstance, whatever it may be, keep praying. Keep asking. Imagine the Lord whispering in your ear, *What do you want?* Stay close to God and count on His grace and mercy in your time of need.

THEOLOGY OF THE NEW DAY

Geraldine had never lived away from her family before. And now it was Christmas, the day before her birthday, and she was still in her first year in China. She had spent the last number of months witnessing horrific sin, opium addiction, and cruel abuse to children. She shared the gospel as she traveled from place to place ministering to the sick, meeting hungry men and women, and struggling with the language.

Geraldine lived in the Hunan province with Hudson Taylor's son and daughter-in-law, Mr. and Mrs. Herbert Taylor, their son, Howard, and their newborn baby girl. Mrs. Taylor was still recovering from the difficult delivery, so Geraldine lent a helping hand, caring for young Howard and the baby. *I've never worked this hard or felt so tired in my life,* she thought. Then, if life was not difficult enough, the baby became ill. Thankfully, there was a nurse to help. But on one fateful, life-altering day, Geraldine was the one who prepared the medicine administered to the baby girl. Geraldine accidentally picked up the wrong medicine bottle. The baby's condition worsened over the next few days, and the newborn died within the week.

The unspeakable had happened. And even though there was no proof the medicine had caused the death, Geraldine was devastated.

She wrote to Hudson Taylor, the baby's grandfather, hoping he, a physician, would somehow be able to assure her that the baby died from the illness, not the medication. Hudson Taylor wisely gave the letter to another son, Howard, who was also a physician and in love with Geraldine. Howard offered such comfort to her that she was renewed and able to go on to a new day in her life. Five years later, she and Dr. Howard Taylor married.

The renewal she received from God early on in China became a vital, necessary experience for the rest of her life. She knew much heartache, years of tireless service for the Lord, and many stupendous victories in His name. God enabled her to carry on in spite of all she endured. Geraldine had learned the secret of the *new day*—God's gracious renewal and restoration for every season of our life. Because she was able to move on to a new day with the Lord, she recovered from numerous miscarriages and lived through the heartbreak of never having her own children.

She never asked, "Why me?" Instead, she opened the Word of God and sought the Lord's divine renewal. She describes how the Lord gave her a new day in one of her quiet times: "Waking later this morning (6:30) after hours of sleeplessness last night, I should have been discouraged—but the Lord Himself made haste to comfort. And oh, what wealth opens up from His Word through this truth applied by His Spirit."[1]

Geraldine experienced renewal for missionary work. She never had a real home of her own because of her missionary work in China. She and her husband moved from place to place, province to province, ministering among the people. More than once, she bordered on burning out in ministry. God gave her the wisdom to pull back, step out of the current, and slow down for renewal and refreshment. Her father, Henry Grattan Guinness, a famous revivalist preacher, wrote a letter to her encouraging rest in a busy ministry. Included in his letter were these wise words, encouraging her to take steps that would lead to a new day for her:

You have in your work been brought face to face with sorrow, want, pain, death, bereavement, miseries of many kinds. You see the world full of them. The problem presses upon your thoughts; it is too much for the weary nerves and heart seen then and thus...When you pitied and loved those poor wanderers and told of redeeming grace, you felt what God is, for He is Love. Dwell then in love, as He is love. Love Him; love all...Lie low, quiet the heart. Turn then away from the patch of darkness close beside you to the blue breadth of azure stainlessness above...Change the theme. Give the brain a rest, give it sleep, give it fresh subjects. Read about other things, about natural history, and whatever interests and pleases you. Go out; let the sweet influences of Nature refresh your tired physical frame, and mental nature too. Let sunshine and breeze, singing of birds, flowers and springtime do their work. Let friendship do its work; talk with others, enter into their concerns. Forget yourself, forget these themes, and the mind shall gain energy and the body health, while the heart rests in Him who rests in His own forevermore.[2]

Geraldine took her father's words to heart and often withdrew for renewal and refreshment. In her new days given by God, she wrote many books, including biographies and missionary works. Her most well-known book, coauthored with her husband, is *Hudson Taylor's Spiritual Secret,* a biography of Hudson Taylor, her father-in-law.

Had Geraldine not learned the secret of the new day, perhaps she would have never written. Maybe she would have even abandoned the mission field. Instead, she triumphed, serving her Lord wholeheartedly all her days. Her books have inspired many missionaries, including Jim and Elisabeth Elliot, to engage in overseas work.

✳

God's grace moves us from one place to another in our walk by renewing our hearts. Those who grow spiritually recognize their need for inner spiritual renewal. When you are renewed, you are no longer stuck, wallowing in your sorrows, fears, anxieties, and despair. Instead, you travel from faith to faith (Romans 1:17) and strength to strength (Psalm 84:7). You will move from wallowing to walking with God in the garden of grace.

How does God's grace renew us? Grace gives us a new day. Though our outer man is decaying, we are renewed inwardly day by day (2 Corinthians 4:16). When you are faced with events that threaten to do you in, God's grace washes through your heart, refreshing you and moving you to a new day. Always look for the new day because it will help you go on in life and not give up.

How can you experience the renewal of God in your own life? What's the secret? God uses His Word to revive, renew, and restore us. In Psalm 119, the psalmist explains again and again that he is revived because of one thing: God's Word at work in his life. Paul encouraged his disciple, Timothy, to live in God's Word because it is inspired by God and is able to teach, reprove, correct, and train him. Renewal and restoration come to you when you sit alone with God and draw near to Him in His Word. The Holy Spirit applies the living Word of God to your hungry, needy heart (Hebrews 4:12).

Perhaps you have often wondered how so many heroes of the faith could have accomplished so much in their lifetimes? They were champions of the Word of God, they relied on the power of the Holy Spirit, and they drew near to God on a regular basis for renewal and restoration. They were clearly established in the knowledge and application of the new day with their Lord. In God's grace, He meets you wherever you are and renews you, thus making each day brand-new. You've heard the phrase "Today is the first day of the rest of your life." In the garden of grace, we can say those words, for God graciously gives us a new day when we walk with Him in the garden of grace. This theology of the new day is vital for our spiritual growth.

We need the grace of a new day when we sin. Unconfessed sin has sunk many a ship that could have continued sailing on the ocean of God's love and grace. Opening the pages of God's Word, we discover that we are forgiven, but we are also encouraged to repent (turn away) from and confess (agree with God about) our sin in 1 John 1:9. To experience the new day, we apply those words, and we confess and repent of our sin. In renewal, we need to receive God's forgiveness, forgive ourselves, and move on to a new day.

Always remember that you are forgiven because of Christ's death on the cross. He paid the penalty for your sin. He does not expect you to carry the sin (Psalm 103:11-12). He already carried it. Corrie ten Boom used to say that when we confess our sins, they are cast into the deepest sea and a sign is put up: No Fishing Allowed. Some sin may bring devastating consequences and a need for restoration of relationships, but God's grace will enable you to face the day and then live on with your Lord. Romans 8:28 still holds true—God causes all things to work together for good for those who love God and are called according to His purpose—regardless of what happens.

We need the grace of the new day when we experience the discipline of the Lord. We learn in Hebrews 12:7-11 that the Lord disciplines us for our good so that we may share His holiness. God's discipline is not punishment, but training. He is making us strong, able to endure even in a fiery trial. In your trial, you can experience the new day when you think of Jesus, who endured, so that you don't grow weary or lose heart. You need to know that the pain of a trial is not going to last forever. God is using your difficulty as discipline to train you up in His ways, make your faith strong, and give you the "peaceful fruit of righteousness" (Hebrews 12:11).

We need the grace of the new day when we experience a great victory. Some successes are so great that they bring down the victor, who never gets past the triumph to move on with God. I believe this is one of the reasons some people, even great men and women according to the world's standards, have fallen into complacency or moral failure.

They could not let go of an enormous victory and continue on in their lives. We need to drink in the words of Philippians 3:13-14 and forget what lies behind, reach forward to what is ahead, and press on toward the goal that God has laid out for us.

My New Testament professor, Dr. Walter Wessel, used to tell us, "After great triumphs often come great times of testing." Great successes are glorious testimonies to the strength and power of God. But we need to adopt Corrie ten Boom's habit of gathering each victory as a rose and presenting the bouquet to the Lord at the end of the day. When we apply Paul's words in Philippians, we won't rest on our laurels. Instead, we will go on with God. There is much work to be accomplished in fulfillment of the Great Commission in Matthew 28:18-20. Jesus is living in you, and He wants to seek and save those who are lost. He will compel you to move on if you want to follow Him and become a fisher of men.

We need the grace of a new day when we fail. Friend, get a grip on the fact that you are not always going to do the right and perfect action, make the right and perfect decision, or be the right and perfect person in the very stuff of life. I've been interviewed on the radio plenty of times, and I've sometimes said things that I would reword if I could. I've missed opportunities to reach out to my friends and family. I've made critical errors of judgment I wish I could take back.

What do we do with failure? We need to drink in the promise of Romans 8:28 and calculate God into our pitiful weakness, realizing He can fill all the empty spaces and weave mistakes and errors into our life stories. Failures have been known to flatten people to despondency and paralyze them for a lifetime. I know of a golfer who was never the same after his failed marriage. I have a friend, however, who drew on God's strength in her broken marriage and continued on to walk in the light of His glory. She has experienced the dawn of a new day, and life has continued on for her. Does God expect us to just lie down and give up in our failure? No. He is a God who encourages resiliency through His Spirit as He renews your heart, refreshes your spirit, and transforms you in His image to be His woman in the world.

We need the grace of a new day when we lose someone we love. In the darkest losses of our lives, we wonder how we can go on. Life will never be the same. I have a friend who suffered the devastating loss of her precious husband. For a time, she wisely withdrew from many ministry commitments to experience restoration from her Lord. She is one of the most godly women I know and such a great example to me.

In the beginning, I asked her how she was doing. She responded quietly, "It's very hard right now. But God is good."

A year later, I noticed that she was present at more ministry events. I asked, "How are you doing these days?"

She said, "Oh, honey, I'm doing great. God is good." She knows the theology of the new day, experiencing God's provision for the deepest needs of her heart.

The new day helps us in all our losses—the loss of a home, finances, loved ones, relationships, hopes, and dreams. Ruth Bell Graham applied the grace of a new day in all the goodbyes she experienced in many decades of ministry with Billy, her husband. She said, "Make the least of all that goes, and the most of all that comes."[3] Those are wise words from one who surely knew a great share of losses in her full and bustling life. Take heart, dear friend, and know that God will move you to a new day in your loss. He will, in His time, turn your mourning into dancing.

We need the grace of a new day when we are working hard and in danger of burnout. We are renewed by Jesus' words in Mark 6:31 and answer His call to come away by ourselves with Him and rest a little while. We realize the need for spiritual rest. The new day gives us wise boundaries that make us strong for the long haul. Then we won't be a one-minute wonder, flickering for a moment before our light goes out. Jesus invites us to move to His rhythm when we are weary and heavy laden (Matthew 11:28-30). He promises rest for our souls when we listen to Him, slow down, and enter His school of the easy yoke and the light burden.

We need the grace of a new day when we are given a new assignment from God. Whether God asks us to do something great or something seemingly easy, we need His renewal for wisdom, strength, and guidance. The promise in James 1:5 assures us that we will receive a generous amount of wisdom from our gracious God. I need the new day every time I write a new book, speak in a radio interview, or teach at a women's retreat. And I also need the new day for tedious responsibilities like paying bills and filing papers. Grace takes us through difficult times and transitions us from one event to another, giving us the new day.

I love one of Kay Arthur's Twitter posts: "Grace = power! Grace calls you to get up, throw off hopelessness, move on through life in faith. When grace calls, grace provides (James 5:11)." Grace truly commands resilience because of its abundant provision. When God daily renews my heart, He helps me approach each responsibility, large or small, as an opportunity from God to serve Him in the strength He supplies.

We need the grace of a new day when we experience spiritual warfare. We have an enemy, the devil, who is also called the father of lies. He will attempt to defeat those who love Christ. His assaults come in many forms. He may attempt to defeat you through antagonism and hatred from others. He may try to convince you of lies that are contrary to the truth of God's Word. God gives you the grace of the new day in spiritual warfare through the Lord's strength and spiritual armor. The full armor of God enables you to stand firm against the schemes of the devil (Ephesians 6:11-18) and leads you to a new day with the Lord in the garden of grace.

We need the grace of a new day when people reject us and our hearts are broken. What will help us when those we love are hurtful, hateful, and simply don't seem to care about us anymore? Renewal during times of rejection comes from God's everlasting love (Jeremiah 31:3). You will experience the new day when you draw near to God and drink in His magnificent, unchanging love. Think long and hard about the words of 1 John 3:1 and experience renewal as the Father bestows His love on you, His child.

You have the wonderful privilege of calling Him *Abba, Father* and can run into the throne room and jump into His everlasting arms. You are the apple of His eye, and He will never forget you. Even if everyone else forgets, He will not forget, for He holds you in the palm of His hand (Isaiah 49:15-16). Jesus knew the pain of rejection and often withdrew to the loving presence of His Father (Luke 5:16).

We need the grace of a new day in illness—either ours or the sickness of a loved one. In these times, our tendency is to live in fear and worry. We need the renewal of Isaiah 41:10, and we find rest in the promise that we need not fear because the Lord is with us. We find new encouragement in God's promises to help us and to hold us in His able and capable hands. I've learned through the fiery trial of my mother's multiple sclerosis and broken neck that overwhelming days may ebb and flow, and they often recede. In the dawn of a new day, we receive new strength to handle difficult decisions and face life's challenges.

We need the grace of a new day with our loved ones, including our husbands, children, parents, and friends. People are part of the race set before us. We are called to love, encourage, and bless those in our lives. How can we reach out to others in the times when we are exhausted, frustrated, or discouraged? Only by the grace of God, experiencing His supernatural renewal by drawing on the power of the Holy Spirit. We need to find strength in Him, acting on the words of Ephesians 5:18 and being filled (controlled and empowered) with the Holy Spirit. His power makes us able and capable, more than we are in our own strength. With the new day we will find that Jesus in us is enough to reach out to those in our lives.

God calls us to this theology of the new day when He says, "Do not call to mind the former things, or ponder things of the past. Behold, I will do something new" (Isaiah 43:18-19). Understanding the reality of new days encourages you to bravely launch out in your life with the Lord. Knowing God will renew, refresh, restore, and revive you brings peace because you can count on Him to make you resilient. Gordon

MacDonald, author and teacher, says resilient Christ-followers stand out from all others. They get stronger, not weaker, in the race of life. He says, "They are committed to finishing strong. They run inspired by a big-picture view of life. They run free of the weight of the past. They run confidently, trained to go the distance. They run in the company of a 'happy few.'"[4] Such a description may seem elusive. You may think, *I would love to be someone like that.* But you need to know that when God renews you in His grace day by day, Christ produces just such a life in you, and every day is a new day.

✳

She was unique. She knew she was not like other women. Deborah certainly carried more responsibilities than any of the men and women in her city. She was married to Lappidoth. But God had gifted her and given her a unique assignment. Had she looked around at other women, she might have thought, *What in the world am I doing here?*

She was a judge over Israel, a female leader in a male-dominated world. Every day was a new day for her. As judge, she sat under a palm tree between Ramah and Bethel. She relied on God to give her wisdom when the men came before her for judgment. She knew He had given her the ability to make decisions. She constantly drew near to God and found Him absolutely faithful to provide her with what she needed. Everyone around Deborah looked to her for a word from God, for she was a prophetess. These were heavy responsibilities for one woman to carry. But Deborah had learned to roll her duties onto the Lord, depending on Him for strength each day.

But today was a new day, for God had shown her His ways and was calling her to a new task. The new assignment was quite daunting, to say the least. She had watched her people cry out to the Lord under the oppression of Sisera, a commander in the army of Jabin, king of Canaan. Now God had shown her His answer. She knew He was asking her to lead the people against their enemies, and He promised,

"I will give him into your hand" (Judges 4:7). What woman had been given such a strategic position over God's people? Deborah was about to receive grace for her new day.

Wisely, she summoned Barak, the son of Abinoam, and said, "Go and march to Mount Tabor, and take with you ten thousand men." But Barak was afraid. She had already sensed his trepidation, but she realized his apprehension more acutely when he told her, "If you will go with me, then I will go; but if you will not go with me, I will not go."

God made Deborah His warrior that day. She responded, "I will surely go with you." And so God's warrior princess went into battle that day, and she found grace to boldly command Barak, "Arise! For this is the day in which the LORD has given Sisera into your hands; behold, the LORD has gone out before you" (Judges 4:14). In the end, the Lord won the battle against Sisera and Jabin, the king of Canaan. The grace given to Deborah in her new day of leadership resulted in peace in the land for 40 years.

✳

Lindsey was so young, only 21, with her whole life seemingly ahead of her. She was a beautiful model, an outstanding student, a tennis player. She had been chosen as one of the Bob Hope Classic Girls the previous year at the Bob Hope Golf Tournament. She had also served overseas in short-term missions and was dating the man of her dreams. Both she and her boyfriend loved the Lord and looked forward to a bright future.

We all remember the day we received the news of Lindsey's diagnosis of sarcoma, a terminal cancer, with a grim prognosis of a very short time to live. I had served side by side in ministry with her mother, Debbie, for many years and had known Lindsey since she was just a young girl of ten. Our church felt as though we were on the front lines of this life-and-death drama, praying fervently for a miraculous healing and encouraging the family with our love and prayers. Every day I logged on to the special website designed just for Lindsey, where we could post messages and prayers. Lindsey's ordeal of suffering became our burden, gladly borne for the sake of our beloved friends in the Lord.

Lindsey was in a battle, and yet she was more concerned about everyone else. But that was Lindsey. She had a heart as big as the world, a bubbly personality, and a charisma that drew people to her. Her hospital room became a meeting place for hundreds of men, women, and children. My friend Conni visited almost every day and would ask Debbie, Lindsey's mother, "What can we pray for?"

Debbie would respond, "Grace for today, Conni. We just need grace for today."

Every day brings new grace to meet new challenges. That's why we need this theology of the new day, for we need God's grace every waking moment. God poured out His grace on Lindsey and her family for life and for death. One night Lindsey prayed, "God, You've given me a great life and blessed me in amazing ways…I'm not afraid. If my days are up, You want me to come home; I'm ready." On July 24, 2008, He ushered Lindsey into His presence, where she basks forever in the warmth of His smile.

I love Debbie's words reflecting her greatest need: "Grace for today." We need to remember that what we had yesterday does not compare with what God will give us today. Every day is a new day, and God offers us adequate, abundant, overflowing grace for new challenges and opportunities.

I received a phone call from a friend who said, "Catherine, I just called because I was feeling discouraged today. I've been standing strong in a battle, and I've seen God accomplish amazing victories in answer to all my prayers. But today I just felt discouraged."

I said, "I'm so glad you called. Tell me what's going on."

She shared many exciting God-sized miracles. After she had talked for about ten minutes, she stopped and said, "Wow! God is really working. I knew if I called, I would get encouraged."

I smiled and thought, *Lord, there's Your grace, giving my friend renewal for the new day through a simple phone conversation.* Sometimes we just need to call a friend to find grace for the day. Whether God uses a book, a conversation, or a worship song, He will find a way to bring you to a new day by His grace.

I think of my friend Jim Smoke, who was diagnosed with a serious yet treatable illness. You would never know he underwent any kind of treatment. I never heard him speak of it. He never skipped a beat except for the day he had a surgical procedure. He is resilience personified and lives out the theology of the new day all the time. I love watching him, listening to him, and drinking in life lessons. I wish I could be more like Jim Smoke. If I have a toothache, everyone knows about it! I am learning more and more to draw on God's grace and live out the theology of the new day.

All we need is grace for the day, the hour, the moment. Grace for the new day, given by God's Spirit, through His promises, gives us hope. When we think it's over, it's never over. For God always has something up His sleeve, so to speak. As we grow spiritually, we learn not to act on the feelings of the moment, but to rely on God's grace to supply the need in His time. Kay Arthur says that grace "enables you to make it...no matter your need, no matter the circumstance, no matter the pull of the flesh or its weaknesses. The Lord is there with His grace, grace sufficient to make it!"[5] Knowing there is always a new day in God's economy, we trust in God's grace to change our feelings, circumstances, and hearts in His time.

Today, as you walk with God in this garden of grace, where do you need the gracious renewal and revival of a new day? Be encouraged, regardless of how much the boat of your life may rock, because your God never changes. He will tether your heart to His promises with His steady hand, and you will find, in the new day, a new strength to go on. And then, dear friend, you will sing a new song to your Lord—a glorious song of praise and joy.

Part 4

THE GLORY OF GRACE

CRAZY FOR JESUS

Anne Graham Lotz's life appeared to unravel before her very eyes. Over an 18-month period she experienced a "cluster of storms" that left her emotionally gasping for breath.[1] All three of her children married in the space of a year. Then her house was torn apart by a hurricane. Her son was diagnosed with cancer. Her mother, Ruth Bell Graham, endured five life-threatening hospitalizations. Finally, her husband's dental office, where he had practiced for 30 years, burned to the ground. How does a woman who knows God, loves His Word, and faithfully serves Him respond when the rug is pulled out from under her? When everything is taken away, one thing remains. One person—Jesus. Anne Graham Lotz shares her response in her book *Just Give Me Jesus:*

> Even now my duties and responsibilities seem overwhelming and my schedule is overfilled. But I don't want a vacation, I don't want to quit, I don't want sympathy, I don't want money, I don't want recognition, I don't want to escape, I don't even want a miracle...Just give me Jesus. *Please!*[2]

Anne did not come by that statement easily, but only through many years of trusting the Lord in the crucible of life. She did not grow up cultivating an ambition to travel the world and teach others about God.

In the busyness of taking care of her own family, she realized she had "drifted from God."[3] She decided to start a Bible Study Fellowship class in her own town, and she agreed to lead it just so others could study along with her. Three hundred women joined the first day, and she continued teaching because she was growing closer to Jesus in the process. After 12 years, she sensed God's call to give His message from His Word to a broader audience. "God made it very clear to me from Jeremiah 1 that He would be responsible for the audience and I was responsible to be obedient to deliver the message He put on my heart."

What was the message God placed on Anne's heart as she spoke to men and women in prisons, stadiums, churches, and seminaries from London, India, and Puerto Rico to the Ukraine and Russia? She focused on one clear message: "We need more of Jesus. Knowing Him intimately is the key to knowing ourselves and finding our purpose in life."

Gospel recording artist Stephanie Kelly lost several friends in a car accident. Following that tragedy, she received news that her six-month-old nephew, Zachary, was having seizures. Her heart's cry mirrored that of Anne Lotz in wanting more of Jesus. Stefanie found her great comfort in Jesus and wrote "I Know He Knows," a song about His ministry to her during that difficult time. It reflects a heart that just wants Jesus:

> I don't know why the flowers bloom and then
>   they fade,
> I don't know when the wind will change,
> I don't know why the love of many will wax cold,
> But I know He knows.
>
> I don't know when the sun will shine or when
>   it hides,
> I don't know when the wave will subside,
> I don't know why it takes a storm to make
>   me grow,
> But I know He knows.

Though my heart may never know the reason
  for the pain,
My eyes, they may only see the rain,
The answers why may never come,
But hope still floods my soul, I don't know why,
But I know He knows.

I don't know why the heavens open wide and cry,
I don't know why the well runs dry,
I don't know how He turns a heart of stone to gold,
But I know He knows.

And though my heart may never know the reason
  for the pain,
My eyes, they may only see the rain,
The answers why may never come
But hope still floods my soul, I don't know why,
But I know He knows.

I don't know why Messiah died for one like me,
I'll never understand His grace,
I'll never comprehend such love in Him alone,
But I know He knows.[4]

Do you need the comfort of knowing Jesus knows today? Do you need more of Jesus in your life? Do you know Him? Is Christ your all? Does He reign supreme in your life? Spiritual growth in grace means Christ rules in you more and more. He fills the landscape of your view in life. No decision, no assignment, no responsibility is accomplished apart from a new Spirit-filled sensitivity to His desires, His attitude, and His person as He lives in you. More and more, as you grow spiritually, you will become aware of Christ living in you. The Holy Spirit always points to Christ, bringing glory to Him. When Jesus promised the Holy Spirit to His disciples, He said, "He will glorify Me" (John 16:14).

Your walk in the garden of grace is with a person—the Lord Jesus. The more you walk and talk with Him, the more you will know Him. That's why Peter encouraged his fellow believers to "grow in the grace and knowledge of our Lord and Savior Jesus Christ" (2 Peter 3:18). Your growth in grace is linked to your growth in knowing Christ. The more you grow in grace, the more you will know Jesus. And the more you know Jesus, the more you will grow in grace.

When I was in seminary, I had the most interesting conversations with my New Testament professor, Dr. Walter Wessel. I miss him, for he is now face-to-face with the Lord. I don't think anyone knows the New Testament as well as he did. God used him greatly as one of the original translators of the New International Version of the Bible. He once told me, "You know, Catherine, I think deeply about some of those verses about Christ, like Ephesians 1:10, 'the summing up of all things in Christ, things in the heavens and things on the earth,' and Ephesians 1:23, 'Him who fills all in all.'"

He looked at me with one of his knowing smiles, as if there was something yet for me to discover. I looked at him with an absolutely clueless expression, for I had no idea what he was talking about. Dr. Wessel loved to pique our interest and set us on an exploration. I never forgot that conversation and have thought about it often in subsequent years. *Why was that thought of Christ filling all in all so profound to my professor, who knew practically everything about the New Testament?*

I think I understand better now, some 20 years later. Christ is supreme. He is the center of everything, so He should be the center and focus of our lives. The writer of Hebrews focused his letter on this one truth: Christ is preeminent and superior to all else. After pointing out many reasons why Christ is better, the author gave his practical application of "fixing our eyes on Jesus, the author and perfecter of faith" (Hebrews 12:2). Again and again, in many ways, through many writers in the inspired Word of God, we see the centrality of Jesus.

I often ask students in my classes and the people I speak to at conferences and retreats, "What would you do if you suddenly heard the sound of a large crowd and the pandemonium of many people coming our way? Suppose the doors fly open and Jesus walks in the room! What would be your first reaction? Would you run to Him? Would you fall on your face? Would you begin to weep? What would you do?"

When I ask those questions and create that scenario in the audience's mind, the room always gets quiet. Why? I believe it is because the presence of Jesus becomes more real to everyone in those moments. Then I always say, "The truth is, He *is* here, even now."

When Jesus is present, everything else fades into the background. Think about His life on earth. Wherever He traveled, huge crowds followed Him. If people knew He was in their area, they wanted to be with Him to hear Him teach and to watch Him perform miracles. What was the attraction? Sherwood Wirt, in his book *Jesus, Man of Joy,* says, "There is only one answer. Jesus was a man of such gladness of Spirit, such freedom and openness and magnetism in His attitude, that He was irresistible. They wanted to be near Him, to catch His Spirit."[5]

Jesus never changes. He is still irresistible in drawing us to Himself. Beth Moore, in her book *Jesus, the One and Only,* shares her deep longing for Christ: "My chief request of God is that He will supernaturally flood my life with an unending, ever-increasing desire for His Son."[6] Our lives should always be drawn to His presence. Jesus lives in us, and when we focus our attention on Him, fixing our eyes firmly on His person and His ways, we will grow closer to Him. And the more intimate we become, the more we will love Him and relinquish control of our lives to Him. When He reigns and rules in our lives, everything else falls into place.

✳

A woman of status and means in Herod's courts usually spent her time in worldly endeavors. Joanna was accustomed to the finer things in life as Chuza's wife. Chuza managed all Herod's vast estates.

Joanna had witnessed firsthand the corruption of power in the hands of Herod, tetrarch of Galilee and Perea. She watched him divorce his wife so he could marry Herodias, his brother's wife. She heard a man named John the Baptist tell Herod, "It is not lawful for you to have her" (Matthew 14:4). How would Herod respond to such criticism? She had seen the look on his face, knowing it meant certain death for anyone who dared criticize him. John was a unique case because he intrigued Herod. Herod kept him safe, for he enjoyed hearing him speak.

Joanna was horrified when Herod swiftly ordered John's execution at the whim of Herodias and her daughter, who had entertained Herod with a pleasing dance. Herodias hated John and wanted him dead, and she got her wish. But in the process, her husband, Herod, was haunted by his evil actions. He could not forget about John, whose words came back to him again and again. And now, he was hearing about a new prophet, one greater than John, named Jesus. New thoughts and fears flooded his mind. Was it John reincarnated? Was it Elijah? Who was this Jesus?

Talk about Jesus was everywhere in Herod's court. Joanna had heard of His miracles. The paralyzed were walking, demons were cast out of possessed women, and blind men regained their sight. No human could perform such wondrous acts. But her interest became personal when she herself began to suffer from an incurable illness. She consulted the best doctors but could not get better. Her pain intensified. And with her pain came a new and deeper obsession with Jesus. She had to see Him and get near Him. Maybe He could heal her.

She knew all about power. It was *who* you knew that got you ahead. She had seen plenty of people capitalize on Herod's power to get what they wanted. But heavenly power—the power of God—presented a new challenge for Joanna. She had no "in" now. She could not approach Jesus in the strength of her husband's name or Herod's. Jesus had no reason to even give her the time of day.

One day, out of desperation, she decided to take a chance. Would

Jesus give her an audience? Through word of mouth, she discovered where He was going to be teaching. She listened to His words from a distance. She did not know anyone who could introduce her to Jesus. The more she listened to Jesus and watched Him healing others, the more she thought about Him healing her. *I know He can heal me. If only I can get close to Him and talk with Him. But who am I? Why would He have any interest in me?*

And just as she was thinking these things, she felt someone next to her. She turned, and there He was. She looked into His eyes with a mixture of shock and excitement. She knew He knew her through and through. She did not have to even say anything. And before she even spoke, it seemed, she felt a power flow through her body. She was healed! Jesus had healed her. As quickly as He had been present with her, now He was moving on, and the crowd was following.

How could one moment and one person alter the course of her life? Yet meeting Jesus changed everything for her. She had only a few minutes to think about what had happened. Some women approached her and introduced themselves to her—Mary Magdalene, Mary the mother of James, and others. All of them shared the same story, "He healed us too. We know exactly how you are feeling right now. We have decided to follow Jesus. Join us. We are a small band of women who are helping Jesus and His disciples. We are learning about the kingdom of God and growing spiritually."

We will never know how Joanna was able to leave her home and the court of Herod. Was she now a widow? Or did her husband become a secret supporter of Jesus? We do know that Joanna joined the small band of women who followed Jesus and financially supported His earthly ministry (Luke 8:1-3). She became good friends with this group of women who also loved Jesus. Oh, what adventures they had experienced with Jesus and His disciples. She knew He was the Messiah. And she was committed to Him for life.

But life with Jesus had taken a dark turn down an unexpected road. Earthly power had clashed with heavenly power. She had experienced both kinds of power and knew God's was greater, yet earthly power had seemingly triumphed. And Jesus was arrested. She watched from a distance, hoping He would work some miraculous expression of His power and defeat Herod, Pilate, and all the religious leaders. But instead, she saw the horrific scourging and Jesus' crucifixion.

Confused and devastated, the women held on to each other, sobbing uncontrollably. Shattered, Joanna and the other women were consumed with a shared desire: "We must give Jesus a proper burial." Joseph and Nicodemus had rushed the embalming process and quickly placed Jesus in the tomb. The women followed to discover the location of Jesus' tomb. They resolved to return after the Sabbath, honor Jesus, and apply the prepared spices.

It was early dawn, the first day of the week after the Sabbath. Their little band of women walked down the path to Jesus' tomb. Things were not as they had been just a few days ago. The stone, too heavy for any human to move, was rolled away from the front of the tomb. They rushed through the opening. "The body of the Lord is missing!" Joanna's mind thought through possible explanations, but none made any sense.

Before she could think beyond the initial reactions, two men in dazzling clothing suddenly appeared. Joanna fell to her knees. All of the women were on their faces when they heard the men speak. "Why do you seek the living One among the dead? He is not here, but He has risen."

After the angels spoke, Joanna remembered Jesus' promise to rise after three days. "We must go tell everyone!" As they ran down the path, making their way to the disciples, they saw a familiar figure. It really was true—Jesus was alive. They grabbed His feet, not wanting to let Him go. "Do not be afraid. Go and take word to my brethren" (Matthew 28:8-10). And so it was that a small group of simple women, including Joanna, were given the distinct privilege of being the first to deliver the news to the disciples and others that Jesus was risen from the dead.

✳

Joanna's life with Jesus is an illustration of God's grace, taking you into the courts of the King, where you see Jesus. Who is this one who now lives in you? As you grow in His grace, you grow intimate with Jesus, who is your life. And you will fall in love with Him, crazy in love with Him. It's true. The more you know Him, the more you love Him. You can't help it. Just imagine the most incredible person you've ever met, and multiply that person's best attributes by the largest figure you can dream up, and you won't come close to how magnificent and wonderful Jesus is. As you enter the courts of the King, whom will you see?

You will see God. Jesus is God incarnate and has explained God to us (John 1:18). Josh McDowell, once skeptical about Jesus, set out to disprove His claims. After all his research and investigation, Josh concluded that it would take more faith to reject Jesus. He discovered that Jesus is indeed more than a carpenter—He is God.

The story is told about a certain kingdom with a handsome prince who was searching for a woman to become his wife and queen of his domain. One day, he traveled through a poor village. As he glanced out his carriage window, he saw a beautiful peasant woman. During subsequent days, he often passed by her and soon fell in love. But he had a problem. How could he seek her hand?

He could command her to marry him, but that was not what he desired. The prince was not interested in a relationship of coercion, but a marriage of love. He could overwhelm her with his splendor and wealth, but then how would he know if she really loved him? Finally he came up with another solution.

He removed his royal robes, put on common dress, moved into the village, and related to her without revealing his identity. As he lived among the people, the prince and the woman became friends. Soon, the young lady loved him for who he was and because he had first loved her.

This is a picture of the gospel. The Prince of Peace Himself, King of kings and Lord of lords, Jesus Christ, set aside His robes of glory, dressed Himself as a commoner, became a human being, and moved into our town, onto planet earth, to woo us to Himself. Francis Chan explains in his book *Crazy Love* that the "wildest part is that Jesus doesn't *have* to love us. His being is utterly complete and perfect, apart from humanity. He doesn't need me or you. Yet He wants us, chooses us, even considers us His inheritance (Ephesians 1:18). The greatest knowledge we can ever have is knowing God treasures us."[7]

When Jesus walked on earth 2000 years ago, He explained God's nature to us, for He is the exact representation of God (Hebrews 1:1-3). The more I read the Gospels, the more I learn about Jesus, and the more I understand God. I understand who this person is who lives in me and who is manifesting a fragrant aroma through me to touch a lost and hurting world (2 Corinthians 2:14). The ministry He had on earth 2000 years ago continues through those He indwells by the Holy Spirit. Let me say that again in another way, for it is profoundly important. Don't miss it. Jesus said that His food was to do the will of God and accomplish His work 2000 years ago, and His desires never changed. He is still at work, seeking and saving the lost in and through willing servants—those who are His disciples and His friends, like you and me.

Who is this one who lives in us and loves through us? I love how one author has written about Christ, helping us remember all He is and has done for us:

> Christ for sickness, Christ for health,
> Christ for poverty, Christ for wealth,
> Christ for joy, Christ for sorrow,
> Christ today and Christ tomorrow;
> Christ my Life, and Christ my Light,
> Christ for morning, noon and night,
> Christ when all around gives way,

Christ my everlasting Stay;
Christ my Rest, and Christ my Food,
Christ above my highest good,
Christ my Well-beloved Friend,
Christ my Pleasure without end;
Christ my Savior, Christ my Lord,
Christ my Portion, Christ my God,
Christ my Shepherd, I His sheep,
Christ Himself my soul to keep;
Christ my Leader, Christ my Peace,
Christ hath wrought my soul's release,
Christ my Righteousness divine,
Christ for me, for He is mine;
Christ my Wisdom, Christ my Meat,
Christ restores my wandering feet,
Christ my Advocate and Priest,
Christ who ne'er forgets the least;
Christ my Teacher, Christ my Guide,
Christ my Rock, in Christ I hide,
Christ the Ever-living Bread,
Christ His precious Blood hath shed;
Christ hath brought me nigh to God,
Christ the everlasting Word,
Christ my Master, Christ my Head,
Christ who for my sins hath bled;
Christ my Glory, Christ my Crown,
Christ the Plant of great renown,
Christ my Comforter on high,
Christ my Hope, draws ever nigh.[8]

The more you know Jesus, the more your life will shine for Him. You will clearly stand out in the crowd, and others will be drawn to Him. A.W. Tozer points out the uniqueness of those who know Jesus:

A real Christian is an odd number anyway. He feels supreme love for One whom he has never seen. He talks familiarly every day to Someone he cannot see. He expects to go to heaven on the virtue of Another, empties himself in order that he might be full, admits he is wrong so he can be declared right, and goes down in order to get up. He is strongest when he is weakest, richest when he is poorest, and is happiest when he feels worst. He dies so he can live, forsakes in order to have, and gives away so he can keep. He sees the invisible, hears the inaudible, and knows that which passes knowledge.[9]

As Jesus lives His life in and through you, He will make you more and more like Himself, conforming you to His image. You will have a heart of compassion, having pity on and giving mercy to others instead of spreading a contentious spirit. You will have kindness instead of severity, bearing others' shortcomings. You will profit another person in some way rather than jealously making war upon the good you see in another.

You will lift up the good in others instead of diminishing it. You will be humble instead of arrogant. You will have the correct estimate of yourself rather than prideful ambition. You will be gentle, accepting God's dealings with you and considering them as good because they enhance the closeness of your relationship with Him. You will endure trials with patience and joy instead of being controlled by an angry temper and flying off the handle. You will trust the Lord instead of protecting your self-interest with disputing, rivalry, and vengeance.

You will bear with the weaknesses and errors of others instead of slandering and speaking against them. You will forgive instead of gossiping and whispering against another. You will put on love instead of causing a negative commotion. The Lord's peace will rule in your heart. The Word of Christ will richly dwell in you. Others will notice that you have been with Jesus, for you will be more and more like

Him, conformed to His image (Romans 8:29). As you grow in grace, people will see that the great exchange has indeed taken place—His life for your life.

✳

Years ago, I was experiencing a bend in the road and a personal spiritual crisis. I was working in utter obscurity in an office, doing simple, mindless tasks that I could accomplish with my eyes closed. I had managed an office in earlier years and had hired others to do this job. It was easy work, though others thought the job was difficult. Coworkers told me, "Wait until our busy season. You'll barely make it through each day." I smiled. They had no idea how many hours I had worked in earlier years. The busy season was a breeze, and I was totally bored. After only weeks, I knew I had to resolve my attitude with the Lord. How do you live life for the glory of the Lord when you are not doing what you truly love to do?

When we find ourselves overwhelmed by a trial and sinking rapidly, we need to take God seriously and find out what He might be up to in our lives. Anne Graham Lotz came to that conclusion in her own crisis: "This time of personal and financial turbulence has served to create a high level of expectation in my heart. Since I know God loves me and is in control of all things, I also know this current round of multiple challenges I'm facing must mean *He is up to something. What is it?*"[10]

I knew in my situation that God was at work in my life, causing me to grow. I knew He was up to something. I just did not know or understand what He was doing. And so I sat down with the Lord and talked with Him about my job. He once again reminded me that life is not about what I do, but about my relationship with Him.

Oh yes—I know, Lord…but I forgot. I guess I didn't really know the way I know now.

And then He reminded me that He has called me His friend (John

15:15). He seemed to be saying, *Let's grow our friendship—I want you to get to know Me better. This job is where we will commune, and it's where I want to be right now in and through you.* I realized I had cultivated an incorrect view about life, working to better my position, even in ministry. And Jesus was reminding me that He wants me to work toward one thing: *knowing Him.* He wanted me to know Him more and more.

My time with Jesus that morning revolutionized my outlook on my job and my life in general. My heart was set on fire as I remembered that He had not forgotten me and, in fact, had especially directed me to this job for the high purpose of knowing Him. I poured myself into knowing Jesus.

Do you know what I discovered? The hymn writer is correct: What a friend we have in Jesus! I studied His character in the Gospels and applied what I learned each day, talking with Him as though He was right there with me. And of course, He *was* with me. I learned that faith in the facts of God's Word resulted in experiencing Him firsthand in my day. Did I always feel Him there? No, but the fact of His presence was more real to me, and I functioned moment by moment in response to those facts. I was leaning in to Jesus' embrace and, as I like to describe it, dancing with Him.

Knowing He is the light of the world meant He is the light in my life. *Thank You, Lord, for brightening my day today. Shine in and through me among my coworkers in this job.*

Knowing He is the bread of life meant He feeds me and provides for me. *Thank You, Lord, that You are my satisfaction and meet the deepest needs of my heart.*

Knowing He is the vine and I am the branch meant He would help me in my work. *Thank You, Lord, that You are with me in everything I do and will supply me with what I need to do this job.*

What I learned in four months at that job was only the beginning of a more intense journey with Jesus, walking and talking with Him throughout the day. He is my life, and I have only scratched the surface of His greatness and glory. Since then I've learned that Jesus walks with people in all walks of life—golfers, accountants, secretaries, actors, plumbers, pastors, and presidents. Because Jesus has risen from the dead, He is alive. And He lives in any who have said yes to Him.

How well do you know Jesus? Is He your best friend? He wants to walk and talk with you even today. Always look for truths about Jesus whenever you open the pages of the Bible. Every page will say something to you about Him. Your goal when you fix your eyes on Jesus is to know and love Him more so that you might grow in the grace and knowledge of Him.

The story is told about a farmer who taught his son how to plow in the field. He hitched up the horse and said to his son, "To plow straight, fix your eyes on that cow at the end of the field." So the obedient son began plowing. The farmer left to do his chores for the day. When he returned, he was surprised to find that his son had plowed in circles rather than a straight line. When he asked his son what had happened, his son replied, "Well, I followed your instructions. But the problem is, the cow kept moving." The good news for us is that Jesus, the object of our attention, never changes. He is faithful and leads us on a straight path as we fix our eyes on Him.

As you walk with Him, following His lead, He will remind you of Himself. One Easter morning I missed a beautiful sunrise. Our backyard has very little view of the sky due to the abundance of foliage. At church later that day, a lady asked, "Did you see the sunrise this morning? It was magnificent!" Her words cut into my heart, reminding me of earlier years in another house, where I used to sit and watch the sunrise. I hadn't seen it. I missed it. Just when I was about to start feeling sorry for myself and launch into a full-blown pity party, the Lord reminded me of something He had shown me about Himself many years before.

I had been sitting in my quiet time in San Diego and had observed a magnificent sunrise. The beauty that morning prompted me to write a prayer to the Lord in my journal, asking for a sunrise in my own life.

Just then, I turned to Luke 1:67-80, my daily Bible reading, and discovered a new name for Jesus: "the Sunrise from on high."

On Easter morning, the Lord reminded me that earthly sunrises will come and go, but He will be with me forever. He seemed to be saying personally to me, *I am your sunrise, more beautiful, more incredible than any earthly thing.*

I responded, *Thank You, Lord. You mean more to me than all the collective wealth and possessions on earth.*

David Bryant, in his book *Christ Is All,* speaks of the supremacy of Christ:

> Everything that matters is reduced to this one Person...He is thoroughly sufficient for the needs of a whole universe. He can satisfy the longings of the nations. He can infuse the saints with the power of resurrection life...He's everything we have. He's everything we need. We can actually make it with Him alone...He belongs fully and equally, in His totality, to all who trust in Him, without exception...He is our destiny. His throne is our home. He is the one with whom we will be preoccupied forever. That's why there is *no other hope* for us to proclaim.[11]

When you realize Christ is supreme, every priority is sifted, and affections are put in their rightful place.

I want to ask you, are you in love with Jesus? Francis Chan speaks of having a crazy love for Christ. Crazy love is opposite of lukewarm affection.

> Lukewarm people are moved by stories about people who do radical things for Christ, yet they do not act...Lukewarm people say they love Jesus, and He is, indeed, a part of their lives. But only a part. They give Him a section of their time, their money, and their thoughts, but He isn't allowed to control their lives...Lukewarm people think about life on earth much more often than eternity in heaven.[12]

The Lord knows your heart. In fact, He spoke directly to the Laod-iceans in western Asia Minor, letting them know He saw their lukewarm hearts. And He proceeded to challenge them to have hearts on fire (Revelation 3:15-16).

Jesus wants our love. And I would venture to say that anyone who isn't on fire for Jesus with an outrageous, crazy love for Him just does not yet know Him intimately. If you're not in love with Him now, set aside time, get alone with Him, open your Bible, rest in His love, listen to Him speak, and gaze at His beauty. Theory will become experience. The academic will become authentic. And the secular will become spiritual. Just see if time with Jesus doesn't set your heart on fire and make you homesick for heaven. Now *that's* real growth in grace.

Jesus continually shows me that He is more than any earthly thing, including a house, a sunrise, or a job. He is always more. *Christ is all.* And because of who Christ is, what He does, and what He says, I am crazy in love with Him.

12

THE FINE ART OF GRACING ANOTHER

Ney Bailey is one of my favorite people in the whole world. I've experienced God's grace every time I've been with her. Marilyn Meberg, one of the Women of Faith speakers, refers to Ney as a "faith connoisseur extraordinaire."[1] Ney has been on staff with Campus Crusade for Christ as a traveling representative for many years. She is the one who taught me all about faith and gave me a deep love for God's Word.[2] I've noticed that Ney is always looking for ways to give out the grace of God to those around her.

Marilyn tells the story of how much she wanted to attend the Chris Evert cup, a professional tennis event that had been sold out for months. And Ney knew how much Marilyn wanted to go. One Tuesday evening, Ney announced, "I'm going to get tickets for Wednesday." Marilyn knew the proposal was impossible. The Sold Out sign meant no more tickets. "I've been talking to God about this, Marilyn, so I'm going to the ticket window early in the morning to see what happens." Marilyn was skeptical about Ney's idea but knew there was no changing Ney's mind. Ney was on a mission, propelled by an indomitable faith in a big God. Marilyn had seen Ney like this many times before. Marilyn's phone rang at 8:13 in the morning. Ney announced excitedly that she had gotten the prized center-court box seats.

199

What a day the two of them shared, watching amazing tennis from their prime position. Marilyn could not stop talking with God. "Thank You, thank You, thank You! You know how I adore tennis…you know how I adore being outside in this gorgeous desert sunshine…I don't quite get it, but thank You, thank You, thank You!"[3]

Ney graced Marilyn that day not only with tennis tickets but also with a new discovery about God. Marilyn often wondered how much God cares about the little things in her life. Later that evening, she talked with Ney about a God who even gives tennis tickets as a grace gift. Ney responded, "I learned years ago not to edit my prayers… Like a father, it pleases Him to give good gifts to His children. And Marilyn, God gifted both of us with a great day of tennis! Our job is simply to unwrap His gracious gift…and enjoy!"

✳

Have you learned the fine art of gracing others the way Ney has? Gracing someone means you listen for God, respond to His leading, and lavish God's grace on that person with rich expressions of His love. Grace gifts can be simple, like a card or a phone call to lunch. Or they can be more extravagant, like a gift wrapped with a big, beautiful bow. Gracing others offers them forgiveness when you have been wronged or extends kindness in the face of deep suffering. You become a vessel of God's glory as His grace flows in and through you. Because grace is unmerited favor, you may give your greatest gifts of grace to those who deserve them the least. Gracing others depends on God, not people, and draws from His inexhaustible storehouse of blessing. Grace givers influence those around them, offering a clear view of God, who lavishes grace on undeserving sinners. The more you unwrap and enjoy God's grace in your own life, the more you will give away to others tangible demonstrations of grace. You can't help it because grace gives and gives and gives some more. And then grace does what it does best—it lavishes a bold touch of God in the life of another. Cathleen Falsani calls such touches "the kick-in-the-pants, clarifying, cosmic-pause-button kind of grace."[4]

The best prescription for the "Poor me," "I'm worried," "I'm afraid," "I'm giving up," or "It's over" feelings that we struggle with from time to time is to find someone in need and give them a good dose of grace. In fact, God promises a new sunrise of light in your darkness and makes you like a watered garden when you give to those who are hungry or afflicted (Isaiah 58:10-11). What will help you give to someone else? Take time to remember God's benefits (Psalm 103:2) and thank God for every gift of grace in your life. Think about the simple things, like air to breathe, a beautiful sunrise, or a friend's smile.

Grace makes you thankful to God, grateful for all He's given you. Even if you are poor monetarily, you still feel rich because of His grace gifts in your life. Grace also makes you sensitive to others' needs. When God ministers to you in particular ways, you begin to wonder, *Does someone else share my need?* You notice the details of others' lives. You just can't help this new sensitivity, for God infuses your heart with a new and deeper love for others. I find myself constantly surprised at the power of God's grace making me reach out to people in my life.

One day, a friend of mine shared that she works so hard in her store that she never has time for lunch. I thought, *What if I brought her lunch today?* The thought and the action were born in the same moment. I quickly drove to one of my favorite restaurants, ordered food I know she likes, and took it to her store at lunchtime. She was serving five customers at once and could barely even say thank you, but I didn't care. I just wanted to grace my friend. And real grace doesn't need anything in return.

Another day I was in a Christian bookstore and saw a beautiful wooden sculpture of a bird with the etched word *Hope.* Instantly, I thought of a recent phone conversation with my mother and a comment she made: "Cath, I just need more hope. I need to remember that God gives me hope."

I grabbed that bird and bought it. When I was in Phoenix visiting my mother, I pulled out my little treasure and said, "Mother, this needs to sit on your desk. When you look at it, remember that God gives you hope. Use this little bird to remind you of all the ways you have hope in your Lord."

With tears in her eyes, she said, "Oh, Catherine, I love this little bird. Thank you. I will look at it often."

I didn't know if the bird would encourage her. You never know what God will use in someone's life. However, in this case, there is no question that the God of grace wanted to pour out a grace gift to my precious mother on that day. Every time I speak with her on the phone, she talks about the "hope bird." She loves it. And God uses that little red bird to remind her of His magnificent, extravagant grace.

I think about the many ways God has graced me through others. My friend Conni graced me early on in my ministry by encouraging me to complete my first book. Few people will truly take your dreams on as their own and encourage you to run your race well. God has graced me with Conni, who loves the Word of God and loves me. She was simply unmoved in her confidence that I would complete my book idea and that she would lead a pilot class. She is an author in her own right, yet she took hours out of her life to encourage me. I received undeserved grace from her, and God used His grace, flowing from the life He so powerfully lives in Conni, to encourage me to become an author. I did finally complete that book and have gone on to write 17 more books. When you become a grace giver, God will multiply your acts of grace to touch the lives of thousands, maybe even millions.

I think of my friend Cindy, who listens to all my big ideas. I am an idea person, and I probably have at least ten ideas a day to encourage others in their quiet time. If I truly listened to all my own ideas, I think I would start to laugh. But Cindy never laughs. She's a grace giver, and one of her gifts is listening enthusiastically to each idea and then brainstorming how we could accomplish my idea. Now truly, if we did everything I dream up, we would need to be 100 people at once.

Her grace gifts to me have helped me develop many of the aspects of Quiet Time Ministries that have encouraged thousands of people and helped them grow in their quiet time with the Lord.

I think of my friend Bev, who recently graced me while I was writing this book. She called and said, "Catherine, how would you like to stay at my house while you write?"

I was blown away because she lives near the coast, right by the ocean. I couldn't have imagined a more inspirational place to write my book. Usually I'm sequestered away at a little hotel, someplace obscure and unpopulated. I said, "Really, Bev? That would be amazing." I thought, *How appropriate that God would grace me through my friend Bev while I'm writing a book about grace.* What a gift she gave me that day, and what an expression of God's grace.

I think of my mother, who graced me in my early years. She would surprise my brother and me with a box of donuts and an early morning drive. We didn't have very much money, but we sure did have fun. And my mother would lavish us with gifts custom designed for us. When we ordered books through the school book club, my mother ordered dozens of books for me. She knew how much I loved to read. But the greatest gift of grace my mother has given me is her love. She has shown her love to me in countless ways. Even now, she sends me e-mails saying, "Catherine, I just want you to know how precious and loved you are." And she always closes with LHKS—our secret motto of affection: love, hugs, kisses, smiles.

God has shown me His grace through so many in my life. My husband graces me every day with big hugs and strong encouragement. My dad graces me with his confident challenges to never give up. My brother graces me with his daily phone calls to say "I love you." My friend LuAnn graces me by visiting my mother and showering love on her. My assistant, Kayla, graces me with her humble attitude and willingness to work hard serving Quiet Time Ministries. My friend Shirley graces me as she organizes my books and edits our quarterly magazine. Paula and Sandy grace me through their help in our office.

Shelley graces me through her tireless service at our church. Our women at church grace me with their love for the Lord. My friends Kelly and Julie grace me with their fervent prayers for me and our ministry. I could go on and on with the multitude of ways God daily graces me. And I am learning how to carry on that attitude in my own life and grace others in both small and large acts of kindness.

✳

The breeze from the Mediterranean filtered in through the open window in the upper room of one of the homes in Joppa. A woman had just died, and her body had been washed and laid carefully on the bed. This was not just any woman, but one known and loved by all. Dorcas was a grace giver. Her acts of mercy and kindness were spread all around with seemingly no one untouched by her love. So great was the outpouring of grief, it seemed the whole town stood at her door. They were waiting for a miracle. Some of the disciples had sent for Peter, who happened to be in a neighboring town. They held out for a miracle from their Lord, conducted through His servant Peter. They knew what Jesus had done during His earthly ministry. Perhaps He would again raise someone from the dead. No one deserved a miracle of grace more than Dorcas, who had cultivated the fine art of gracing hundreds through her own life and ministry.

Dorcas, also known as Tabitha, had been a disciple of Jesus. She had said yes to following Jesus and was filled with a hunger and desire to learn His ways and grow in her love for Him. She also discovered a deep passion to touch others through acts of kindness. She loved nothing more than pouring out the grace of Christ to people who could do nothing to earn her gifts. Such deeds were effortless and small in comparison with the grace she had received from her Lord.

But Dorcas became very ill, suddenly it seemed. One minute she was actively ministering to others, and the next moment she was lying in bed, fighting for her life. She was helpless in her sickness and could only receive the kind care of some of the widows in Joppa. She felt herself slipping away physically, and finally, one day, she breathed her last. So now her body rested in the upper room of her home. And all the people were waiting. The widows downstairs wept at the loss of their precious friend. Evidence of her active life was everywhere in the home—garments she had made, tunics for the poor…stacks of them ready to be given away.

Two men traveled swiftly to Lydda, 11 miles southeast of Joppa. They brought the message to Peter from all the other disciples in Joppa: "Do not delay in coming to us." They implored him to come. Perhaps Peter was reminded of the day Jesus went to the home of Jairus and raised his 12-year-old daughter from the dead, saying, "Stop weeping, for she has not died, but is asleep" (Luke 8:52). Peter, along with James and John, had witnessed the miracle firsthand. People had laughed at Jesus' words. But they stopped laughing when Jesus took the child by the hand and said, "Child, arise." A miracle came to the house of Jairus that day, for his little girl rose from the dead.

When Peter arrived in Joppa, he was taken to the upper room. Looking at Dorcas's body lying there on the bed, perhaps he saw in a flash the dead body of a little girl years before. If Jesus raised her then, maybe He would give a miracle of grace to Dorcas and all her friends on this day. For Peter knew the power at work in him was not his own, but belonged to Christ Himself.

Peter sent everyone out of the room and shut the door. Now he was alone with his Lord. Kneeling down, he prayed to his Lord and Master. Calm and assured, he turned to the body and spoke as though she were there: "Tabitha, arise." She opened her eyes, looked at Peter, and sat up. He held out his hand and helped her out of bed. Peter saw the grace of his Lord in action. He called out to everyone in the house. They came in the room and were met with God's miracle—their beloved Dorcas was alive and well! Word spread quickly throughout Joppa, and many believed in Jesus. Once again, one gracious act multiplied to many, who were saved by grace.

✳

What will make you a grace giver like Dorcas? First, you need to know and experience God's grace in your own life. Dorcas was Jesus' disciple, and you also must also step out of the crowd and say yes to follow Jesus. Then ask God to show you new opportunities every day to grace someone else. Grace breaks down barriers, especially with those in your life who never seem to give in return. Peter, in his little letter on how to suffer, offers instructions in grace giving. He says, "To sum up, all of you be harmonious, sympathetic, brotherly, kind-hearted, and humble in spirit; not returning evil for evil or insult for insult, but giving a blessing instead; for you were called for the very purpose that you might inherit a blessing" (1 Peter 3:8-9).

If you will be a grace giver, you will learn how to give a blessing to those around you in spite of their own actions toward you. Peter specifically lists ways to give a blessing, especially to those who are evil or insulting. Clearly there are no grudges or resentments in grace. But don't you find your greatest difficulty giving grace to people in your life who just don't deserve it? Let's admit it—sometimes people push our un-grace button. But remember, you don't deserve grace either. For you are a sinner, and you received grace and mercy from Jesus when you were His enemy (Romans 5:8-10). When you give a blessing instead of an insult to others, you don't need to *feel* grace, but *give* grace and *be* grace to them. Be a grace walker and not just a grace talker. How then can you give grace to someone who is antagonistic or hurtful? Peter shows us the way

The first quality Peter mentions to give a blessing is being harmonious. You can offer harmony to others by putting yourself in their shoes, imagining what they must be thinking. Paul also encourages this oneness with others when he refers to "being of the same mind" (Philippians 2:2). You stop and take time to share the attitude of someone else. Stepping into the shoes of another person for a moment will totally change the way you treat that person. What a gift of grace you give to obstinate, rebellious people when you take a moment and wonder, *Why are they acting that way? What could possibly cause them to treat me and others with such harsh, antagonistic words?*

Years ago, I tried stepping into the shoes of someone who had spoken harshly with me over a substantial period of time. I stopped one day and thought, *Where is this person struggling? Why in the world is there such resentment and bitterness?* I realized that squelched dreams and lots of talent were locked away in that precious one's heart. The hurtful attitude truly was not about me, but a wrestling within. Instead of acting hurt, I asked God to give me the ability to liberally give out His grace. I looked for opportunities to grace that one. Many years later now, I don't even remember the antagonism, for it is completely gone.

The second quality Peter mentions is sympathy—another gift of grace you can give to others. This attitude of compassion shares others' situations. Sympathy means you enter in to their challenges or joy. You share in their feelings. What a gift you give to other people when you share in their deepest feelings about life. When I am writing a book, I am so encouraged when I receive an e-mail from my assistant, Kayla, asking, "How's the book coming?" She graces me with a sympathetic heart, sharing my joys and also my concerns in ministry.

Next, Peter encourages us to love others as brothers. We grace people in our lives when we recognize them and treat them as family. And in fact, if the people we are gracing are Christians, they *are* part of the family of God. How would you love your dearest sibling? I think of my own brother, Robert. He and I are very close. Very recently, he said, "Cath, if you ever need encouragement or anything at all, just call me." Sometimes he writes to me and says, "Cath, I'm so proud to be your brother." Brotherly love that encourages and admires is a rare gift of grace. But when you give the "brotherly love" gift, in God's time you will see extravagant grace melt even the toughest hearts.

Another way to grace people is by offering kindness to them. This grace gift means you feel deep concern and care for them. Your grace gift becomes an action toward the grace recipient. I think of my friend Julie, whose kindheartedness grew into a big grace gift to young women who were pregnant and considering abortion. Her idea for a Crisis Pregnancy Center became reality, and she has seen literally hundreds of babies' lives saved and young women coming to Christ.

Finally, your humility enables you to give grace to others. Humility allows you to step outside of yourself. Instead of preoccupation with self, you are preoccupied with God and His grace. Have you ever met people who are just full of themselves? You talk with them, but they never hear your words. Humility gives the gift of a listening ear and an interested spirit. Jesus is the most humble one you will ever know. And the more you are with Him, the more humble you will become. He even encourages you to enter His school and learn from Him because He is gentle and humble in heart (Matthew 11:29).

Evangeline Booth grew up in an atmosphere of grace, the daughter of General William and Catherine Booth, founders of the Salvation Army in London in 1878. They were rich in God's grace, filled with a passion to rescue "vast, unmanageable masses of sunken people" in London.[5] Evangeline was accustomed to working in the slums as a teenager, so she was well-acquainted and sympathetic with the poor and needy.

In 1904, at the age of 39, Evangeline became commander of the Salvation Army in the United States. She was respected and admired by all for her confidence and commitment. Completely selfless, she chose never to marry in order to serve the Lord in her place of calling. She was a grace giver 24/7, offering compassion and the smallest kindnesses daily to the poor and lonely in their deep suffering. Because of one person's wholehearted commitment to giving grace, the Salvation Army grew and was firmly established as a ministry to thousands of needy people in the United States.

Whom can you grace in your life today? When you grace others, you give a blessing, a gift completely independent of circumstances. Your desire to grace others will grow as you walk in the garden of grace with your Lord. And who knows, perhaps you will have a ministry of grace like Dorcas or like Evangeline Booth, whose life impacted thousands. God's grace given to people draws them to Christ, where they can experience the greatest wealth of all, the blessing of a relationship with Him.

DREAMING GOD'S DREAMS

A middle-aged lady walked out on the stage, confidently facing the judges for a talent search television program. "How old are you? asked one judge.

She smiled defiantly and declared for all to hear, "I'm 47."

The judges rolled their eyes. Not another loser. How could they endure this day? The judge asked with a smirk, "Okay, so what's the dream?"

She said, with deep passion from years of living with her dream, "My dream is to be a professional singer." Audience members tried to stifle their laughter. This woman was the last person who could be a professional singer.

"Why hasn't it worked out before?"

She replied from the heart, "I've never been given the chance before, so here's hoping it will change." People in the audience were rolling their eyes and scoffing as if to say, "This woman is living in a dream world. She is unbelievable."

"Who would you like to be successful as?"

She knew her object of admiration. She had watched her on television many times and practiced in front of the mirror to sound just like her. "Elaine Page," she said confidently, citing the famous British musical theater star.

Now everyone was laughing.

"What are you going to sing?"

"'I Dreamed a Dream' from *Les Misérables*."

The judges and the audience braced themselves for something hilarious.

The music started, and Susan Boyle began to sing. Shock ensued as her unexpectedly clear and beautiful voice resonated through the performance hall. And the rest is history. The crowd cheered in the presence of one who towered above them all with the voice of an angel. That day Susan Boyle achieved her dream and began her journey as a professional singer.

One aspiring writer watched Susan Boyle sing and picked up an old, unfinished manuscript, dusted it off, and started working again with an all-consuming passion. His old dreams had resurfaced. Here's part of what he wrote:

> Do you remember where you tucked that old, tattered dream? Go look for it as soon as you get up from the computer. We're all in Start Over mode, anyway…Right now, when we're all groping about for a life-preserver, nothing is too silly, too outdated, or too impossible to happen. The Mariners are 6-2. It was 70 degrees last week. The trees are in bloom. And your dream is still there, right where you left it. Go. Grab it. Polish it up. Make it Fly.[1]

Watching Susan Boyle sing in that audition helps everyone remember their own significance and beauty, despite outward appearances. Hidden in the common is utter magnificence, like gold in the dust. Others may think we are worthless, but their opinions are meaningless in the face of God's glorious design. Just think, Susan Boyle sang with her magnificent voice for 47 years in utter obscurity. Then one day, in a brief, shining moment, the world was given a glimpse of what God had enjoyed all those years. And the world cheered, drinking in the wonder of the music.

✳

Everyone is filled with some kind of dream. What's your dream? Christians are given the special grace to carry God's dreams and desires in their hearts. When you walk in the garden of grace with your Lord and grow in your relationship with Him, you will be filled with His dreams—God-given ideas to fulfill in your lifetime and strategies for influencing others now and in the future.

David spoke of God's dreams when he said, "Delight yourself in the LORD, and He will give you the desires of your heart." David was not saying that God always gives you what you want. Instead, he was stating that when you delight in the Lord, you are filled with God-given desires. He continued on to say that your commitment and trust in the Lord results in the fruition of God's plans and purposes for you (Psalm 37:4-5).

David prayed in Psalm 25:4, "Make me know Your ways, O LORD; teach me Your paths." You are given the privilege of knowing God's ways and sharing in His work. He will even tell you the secrets of His heart. David said that the secret of the Lord is for those who fear Him (Psalm 25:14). This secret is intimacy with God and sharing God's heart.

When you share God's heart, you understand more what He wants to do in and through you. You begin to experience His great love for undeserving people. You see His willingness to go to great lengths to save sinners. In His heart, you see the sacrificial love that sent Jesus to the cross to pay the penalty for sin that you might be saved. You observe an unusual love, a severe mercy, in your God. You may not always understand what you see in God, especially when you see a heart pleased to crush His Son, whom He loves. This love moved the Savior to suffer intense anguish and bear the iniquities of others in order to see their justification (Isaiah 53:10-12).

What do you learn from this eternal perspective of God's desires and dreams? His ways are higher than your ways (Isaiah 55:8-9). When you live in the light of His grace, you will find yourself filled with unusual dreams, including some that may not make sense to the world.

Embracing God's big dreams and desires focuses your life on Him and not yourself. Your goal as you walk with God is to discover who God is, what God does, and what He says. This will lead you to understand your purpose for living—to glorify God in everything you do—and to accomplish the specific assignments God has for you. Paul says that you are God's workmanship (Ephesians 2:10). I like to think of us as trophies of grace.

But Paul continues on, telling us that we are created for "good works, which God prepared beforehand so that we would walk in them." I feel like jumping up and down when I read that! In that little statement about God's preparation of good works, we see something big, something huge, in God's mind. God has a plan for you. And He has specific ideas in mind of what He wants you to do. When you walk closely with your Lord in the garden of grace, you will be led by God's Spirit into His plan for your life (Romans 8:14).

I specifically remember the early days in my walk with the Lord when I was filled with a desire to write. I wrote thoughts and insights in my journal. I wrote ideas on pieces of paper. I wrote stories in notebooks. I was writing, writing, always writing. But why? For what purpose? To what end? Words just seemed to flow whenever I put pen to the paper. I had no connections with publishers and no firm idea for a book. When I joined the staff of Campus Crusade, I used my writing skills to design newsletters for my financial support team. And I continued to write my thoughts in my journal as I studied God's Word.

When I attended seminary, I wrote theological treatises with every new assignment. I remember my New Testament professor commenting on one paper, "It's a bit long, but we'll forgive you for that." He gave me an A-plus, a rarity from Dr. Wessel. I treasured that grade so much that I framed it and hung it in my office to remind me always to give my best when I write.

My desire to write did not fade away but instead grew with each passing day as I walked with the Lord. When dreams and desires grow in the context of your thriving relationship with the Lord, Psalm 37:4 is being fulfilled in you, and God is filling you with His desires for your life.

I also clearly remember the day I realized I needed to design a website for Quiet Time Ministries. I walked into a software store, bought Web design software, and taught myself how to build a website. The layout of the website was obvious in my mind. I attribute that clear picture to the Lord. I wrote numerous articles online for the website, using my desire to write as a way to reach others worldwide. I was floored when people wrote to me from places like Africa and Australia, asking if they could use my articles to train others.

I remember the day God gave me the idea for *Pilgrimage of the Heart*, my first book of quiet times. The organization for this book was so clear in my mind that I wrote three chapters in one week. Now, I don't normally write nearly that quickly. And since that time, I've been known to labor many days over a page in a book. But when God is empowering us with His Spirit for His work, sometimes He does extraordinary feats for His glory. I read somewhere that A.W. Tozer wrote *The Pursuit of God* on a train trip. Pretty powerful writing indeed!

I share my own journey of dreaming God's dreams to encourage you to pursue the ideas God is placing in your heart. God may not necessarily use all your gifts and talents to achieve what others think you should accomplish. He may give you a higher calling instead! Only after I became a Christian did writing become a passion, blossoming into a God-given dream to someday write a book. Since that time, I've written many books, and I'm dreaming up more even now. When we walk with God in the garden of grace, we can count on Him to lead and guide us. And listening for His guidance and then responding to Him is part of our growth in Him. The result will be a life of grace used for His glory.

Bruce Wilkinson carried his own dreams of influencing people, yet he was overwhelmed with the fear of public speaking. As Bruce grew spiritually, he learned to trust God when he walked out on stage to speak. God has used him to speak to audiences of millions as a result. Bruce Wilkinson is an example of how God fills one with a dream and then gives the strength and supply to carry out the dream.

✳

Samuel watched as the men entered the place of sacrifice. Only he knew that it was more than a religious ceremony. Soon he would anoint a new king. And he was afraid for his own life. *How can I go? If Saul hears it, he will kill me.* But Samuel really had no choice. God had told him to go. And he knew that the Lord had sought out for Himself a man after His own heart and had appointed him as the ruler over His people. And so now, Samuel may have wondered, *Who is God's choice for king? Who is this man after His own heart?* He would soon find out.

He looked at Eliab, the oldest son of Jesse, a striking young man, and thought, *Surely this is the Lord's anointed!* He waited for God's confirmation. Instead, God gave Samuel a lesson in vision and discernment. And consequently, Samuel gained a glimpse into God's heart. God told him, "Don't judge by his appearance or height, for I have rejected him. The Lord doesn't see things the way you see them. People judge by outward appearance, but the Lord looks at the heart." One by one, each son of Jesse passed in front of Samuel. None was God's choice, yet God had said His anointed was a son of Jesse. A new thought came to Samuel.

"Are these all the sons you have?" asked Samuel.

"There is still the youngest," Jesse replied. "But he's out in the fields watching the sheep and goats."

And then Samuel knew God's choice. Not the obvious, but the obscure. Not the impressive, but the unimportant—at least in the world's eyes. A man who clearly was famous with God, but not with man. His father, Jesse, hadn't even thought of him in answer to Samuel's original invitation. He was the youngest, only a boy, and nothing much to think about. When Samuel laid eyes on handsome young David, he heard God say, "This is the one, anoint him."

God had heard his songs, prayers, dreams, and hopes for his life. He had seen David's courage and valiant trust in Him in the face of great danger. And what God saw was enough for Him. He loved David's heart. David chased after God's will and His ways in rare fashion. And out there in the fields with the sheep and the goats, God had trained His future king in many of the finer points of leadership. Now it was time for the world to experience what God alone had enjoyed. David, the man after God's own heart, would rule over His people with grace, love, and wisdom, bringing great glory to God. David the shepherd became the great King David, ruler over God's people for more than 40 years.

God's plan for David included ruling over His people as the King of Israel. And though He filled David's heart with that dream, it did not come to pass easily. David's life was in danger for many years before he became king. More than once, he wanted to give up. He learned to trust God in the trials, hope in God's promises, and wait for God's guidance. Finally, one day, God brought His plans and purposes to pass for David and made him ruler over Israel.

When God fills your heart with a dream, He may not fulfill it in the ways you expect. Trusting God is the only way to carry God's dreams in your heart. And part of that trust is to lay aside the need to understand what God is doing (Proverbs 3:5-6). Instead, rest in the comfort of knowing that God knows. And knowing that God is about His business in your life and is carrying out His plans becomes enough. And then maybe God will say about us, *She is a woman after my own heart. She will do everything I want her to do* (Acts 13:22).

✳

Lilias Trotter was raised in an environment of culture and beauty. She learned from her mother early on to appreciate a wide range of topics from art and gardening to geology and botany. Her parents were Christians, and she grew up with a strong faith in Christ. Something happened early on to shape her walk with the Lord. When she was 12, her beloved father, Alexander, died. His death served to drive her into the arms of her Lord. When other children were playing, Lilias was often praying in her room. In addition to her special, deep love for the Lord, Lilias also had an unusual artistic ability. With her eye for beauty, she could sketch and draw with ease. What would God do with so much talent in one person?

Lilias was influenced by two towering personalities in her life: Hannah Whitall Smith and D.L. Moody. Hannah Whitall Smith, a well-known Bible teacher, served as a role model for Lilias. And D.L. Moody personally trained Lilias to counsel those who responded in his evangelistic meetings. God gave Lilias a strong desire to serve Him. Once she caught the excitement of seeing Christ change lives, everything else paled in comparison. She loved to win others to the Lord and worked tirelessly at the YWCA.

One trip sifted her affections and led her into God's plan for her life. When she was 23, Lilias accompanied her mother and sister on a trip to Europe. While they were in Venice, her mother discovered that John Ruskin, the great artist, was also in the city. Mrs. Trotter sent Ruskin a set of Lilias's watercolors along with a note requesting his opinion and describing Lilias's lack of training. In the note she admitted that she was "quite prepared to hear that he does not approve of them."[2] He tried to restrain his excitement at Lilias's natural artistic ability. He personally showed the three women the art of Venice and invited Lilias to become his art student. He felt she would become a world-class artist and said she was one of the best artists of the nineteenth century.[3]

For three years Lilias studied with Ruskin. She loved drawing and painting but also was consumed with ministering to the underprivileged in the streets of London. Her art tutor was frustrated with what he viewed as her extracurricular ministry activities. Finally, Ruskin set before Lilias a decision between art and ministry. She prayed, "Lord, make my calling clear." She wrote to a friend, "I know that I have no more to do with the gift than with the colour of my hair...I need prayer to see clearly God's way."[4]

She knew her art could be used for the glory of God, but she concluded after much prayer, "I see as clear as daylight now, I cannot give myself to painting in the way he [Ruskin] means, and continue still to 'seek first the kingdom of God and His righteousness.'"[5] She realized that she could still appreciate art and beauty and wholeheartedly serve her Lord. After she decided not to give herself up to art as a disciple of Ruskin, she still continued her friendship with him as well as her art. However, she now experienced an "independence of soul" she described as "the liberty of those who have nothing to lose because they have nothing to keep. We can do without anything while we have God."[6]

Focusing on Jesus and following His lead in her life were Lilias's priorities.

> It is easy to find out whether our lives are focused, and if so, where the focus lies. Where do our thoughts settle when consciousness comes back in the morning? Where do they swing back when the pressure is off during the day?...Dare to have it out with God...and ask Him to show you whether or not all is focused on Christ and His glory...Turn your soul's vision to Jesus, and look and look at Him, and a strange dimness will come over all that is apart from Him.[7]

What an important step in Lilias's spiritual growth in the garden of grace. She followed Christ into His plan for her life, one that combined all He had worked into her life, including her artistic ability. After hearing a missionary speak of ministry in Algeria, North Africa, she was burdened to reach the Arab world with the gospel of Jesus. Nine months later, she sailed for Algiers with "a strange glad feeling of utter loosing and cast upon God."

Lilias's dream was to live and work among Arabs and lead them to

Christ. She first set out to learn Arabic. When she arrived in Algiers, she moved to the French quarter because she could speak French. She faced many obstacles. How could she and her fellow workers reach Arab women who were secluded in homes that were closed to outsiders? One way was to befriend children, who would then take them to meet their mothers.

Lilias was burdened for the women in Algiers and dreamed of how she could reach them with the gospel. She knew traditional methods could never work in this environment. She discovered that God empowered her to developing unique ways to reach these precious souls with His message. She used a combination of literature and art and love to form classes like embroidery and even Bible study. She and her fellow missionaries did not see quick results, but they continued reaching out in faith. Lilias wrote, "Time is nothing to God—nothing in its speeding, nothing in its halting—He is the God that inhabiteth eternity."[8] She often said, "*He* knows what He would do." She firmly believed in waiting on God for Him to accomplish His work in and through her even if the results appeared after she stepped into heaven.

Five years after she and others arrived in Algiers, they knew the language well enough to move into the Arab district of the city. Sensing the oppression, Lilias felt as if praying all day long would hardly meet the existing needs. Every morning, she walked to a quiet place in Fortification Woods, five minutes from her house. There, from 7:15 to 8:30, she studied Scripture and texts from the devotional *Daily Light* to hear God's voice. She remarked, "It is so delicious on these hot spring mornings, and God rests one through it for the whole day, and speaks through all living things. Day after day something comes afresh."[9]

Her exquisite eyes of faith drank in the beauty of creation, and she filled her diaries with paintings of lessons she learned from her Creator and His beauty. She wrote, painted, and sketched in her many diaries. She created and published booklets from an Arab point of view, complete with writing and illustration. She wrote stories and parables with beautiful drawings and Arab-style borders for the pages. In all her writing and painting, she constantly invited others to "come and look" so they might truly see the unseen with "heartsight" as well as eyesight.

Lilias and her coworker Blanche Haworth founded the Algiers Mission Band, which later became the North African Mission and in 1987 joined the Arab World Ministries. How could two women accomplish so much? They were single-minded and clear about their purpose, and they trusted God to provide for them.

Lilias enjoyed the blessings of a few close friends. One dear friend was Amy Carmichael, who shared her love for God and radical obedience to Christ in ministering on the mission field. Amy enjoyed Lilias's encouragement through at least two of her devotional books, which she sent as personal gifts: *Parables of the Cross* and *Parables of the Christ-Life*.

Lilias Trotter was once described as "beautiful to feel near...It was the stillness of strength, the white heat of iron from the furnace."[10] People loved her quiet manner. After 40 years of ministry in Algiers, Lilias lay in bed dying, surrounded by her Algerian Mission Band and singing "Jesus, Lover of My Soul." She looked out of the window, lifted her hands, and exclaimed what she saw: "Yes, many, many beautiful things." She was buried in the place where God had called her to serve most of her life—North Africa.

Others have said that the will of God will never lead you where the grace of God cannot keep you. God will sustain you, as He did Lilias, in all His leading in your life. God filled Lilias Trotter with His dreams and used her artistic ability to reach women in North Africa with the gospel of Christ. Only God could know that He was going to move His exquisitely sensitive and highly cultured servant to the far side of the world and use her gifts for His glory.

Dreaming God's dreams does not mean achieving fame or fortune, but it does mean you live in the audience of God with one ambition—knowing and loving Him. People who live in the audience of God are able to see beyond the here and now all the way to eternity. Some who are dreaming God's dreams may live in obscurity but are famous in heaven. They are "unknown yet well-known" (2 Corinthians 6:9).

So often we equate fame with value, significance, and importance. This attitude has pervaded even the Christian culture, in which many people still push to become known. We don't need to grow more famous in the world. We need to be more famous with God. And how can that happen? We need to cultivate our intimate relationship with Him and then walk faithfully with Him. God may increase the boundaries of our influence, but the scope and sphere of our ministry is His choice, not ours. And if He is the only audience, with no one else looking on, then living for His eyes only and for His glory is more than enough.

God has given you a unique brilliance, beauty, and giftedness. He will fill your heart with His dreams. Hold your head high, my friend, and love and serve the Lord with all your heart and soul. Be faithful to Him and cultivate the perspective of living in His audience, for Him and Him alone—unknown yet well-known. Then leave the results with God. If, in the course of your journey, He leads you to accomplish your life work for His eyes only, you will have a great reward in heaven, for God sees all you do in secret and promises a reward (Matthew 6:1-6). If He chooses to pull up the shades and give the world a glimpse of what He enjoys, then pray for an extra measure of grace and power to wholeheartedly love and serve Him.

I think about how Lilias's paintings graced God's presence more than man's eyes. Some of her beautiful paintings lie buried in a print room of a museum in Oxford, England, filed in a long cabinet of an art collection. Lilias may have enjoyed very little earthly admiration, but she did have the smile of God. What more could one desire than being well-known by God Himself? And the brightness and satisfaction of His smile is worth more than thousands of cheering voices on earth. Very few know of Lilias Trotter, and only in recent years have her paintings and artwork come to light. Yet she was faithful, and God used her for His glory.

✳

Two Moravian men heard about a slave colony in the West Indies. No one was allowed to approach the island, so these two men offered themselves as slaves for the rest of their lives so they could preach the gospel to others on that obscure island. Unknown yet well-known. Two other Moravians volunteered to go into a leper colony in Africa, where no one was allowed to enter and return, just to present Christ to the inmates of that colony. Unknown yet well-known. Those Moravians formed a motto reflecting their sacrificial service: to win for the Lamb that was slain the reward of His suffering.

Not everyone is called to leave home and travel to the far side of the earth. Some are called to service in their own homes, perhaps to be unknown yet well-known. May you share God's heart, grow intimate with Him, and dream His dreams. Live in the light of His smile, not man's recognition. Only God knows what He will do in and through your life. And He will lead you in His time, in His way, for His purposes, through a myriad of paths He designs. The secret is to draw near *to* Him, grow in your relationship *with* Him, and thrive *in* Him as you live in His garden of grace. And perhaps God will pull up the shades and give others a glimpse of His glory in you. But you may never notice the recognition, for your eyes will be fixed on God's smile and heaven's applause. So make every effort, my friend, to dream God's dreams and live by His grace for His glory.

CHOCOLATE DRINKING FOUNTAINS

I knocked at the door of the group home where my mother lives. The owner of the home opened the door and said, "Hello, Catherine, come in."

I could tell by the look on her face that something had happened. When she hugged me, I asked, "What's wrong?"

She burst into tears and said, "Oh, Catherine, one of our residents is dying. And two others have died in the last two weeks. I'm just heartbroken. I love them so much."

"I'm so sorry. I pray that the Lord gives you His strength and grace right now." I hugged her again.

I walked down the hall toward my mother's room. I could hear voices in one of the other rooms. I peered through the doorway and saw the daughter sitting on her mother's bed and the husband sitting in a chair nearby. I thought, *Here we are, in a real life-and-death trauma with these people. The daughter is about to lose her mother, and the husband is about to lose his wife. And the woman is about to step into eternity.* I found out that these people knew the Lord and that someone had come to pray with them. I was struck with the enormity of the moment for three strangers in a room next to my mother's.

I walked on down the hall, and there was my mother, sitting in her wheelchair, facing the door and waiting for me. Her eyes lit up just seeing me approach, and she opened her arms wide to hug and kiss me. I held her close for a few moments. "Oh, Catherine, I'm so happy to see you. I'm so glad you're here."

"Mother, I just found out that the lady in the next room is dying."

"Yes, I know. It's very sad."

"But Mother, the lady knows the Lord. The family prayed together in the room just a while ago."

Mother and I just looked at each other for a few moments, both caught up in the profound nature of the drama of life and death taking place just next door. Then I got an idea that was so out of the box that I almost rejected it. My mother's favorite hymn is "It Is Well with My Soul." The words always comfort her heart in troubled times.

"Mother, what if you and I sing 'It Is Well with My Soul'? What if we sing it right here and now, softly, as a prayer for this hour in all of our lives?"

"Oh, Catherine, let's do it!" She was my copartner in ministry, as always, ready for the next new God-given idea. And so, without any fanfare, we began singing softly and with feeling the words written by a man who had lost his beloved daughters at sea many years ago:

> When peace like a river attendeth my way,
> When sorrows like sea-billows roll;
> Whatever my lot, Thou hast taught me to say,
> "It is well, it is well with my soul."
>
> My sin—oh, the bliss of this glorious thought—
> My sin, not in part but in whole,
> Is nailed to the cross, and I bear it no more,
> Praise the Lord, praise the Lord, O my soul!
>
> And Lord, haste the day when my faith shall
> be sight,
> The clouds be rolled back as a scroll;

The trump shall resound, and the Lord
    shall descend,
Even so, it is well with my soul.

It is well with my soul,
It is well, it is well with my soul.

When we finished singing, Mother and I hugged, holding on to each other for some time. Then the owner of the house came in my mother's room. "I heard you singing. It was beautiful. Thank you."

As Mother and I left the house to go to lunch, I said, "We'll be praying for you and the family today."

"Thank you, Catherine. I love you both."

Later, riding in the car with my mother, brother, and niece, we talked about what had happened. Kayla, our resident eight-year-old theologian, said with great conviction, "Well, she will be in a much better place than here."

I said, "Is that so, Kayla?"

"Oh yes. You know why?"

"Why?"

"Well, in heaven, everything is much, much better. Even the drinking fountains are amazing."

"Oh?" I responded.

"Yes, didn't you know? In heaven, the drinking fountains don't have water. They have chocolate. You get to drink chocolate all day long. Mmmmm."

"So there are chocolate drinking fountains in heaven?"

"Yes, and you know what else?"

"What?" I asked, hardly able to wait to hear what else I was going to learn about heaven.

"When it rains, it rains chocolate chip cookies. So, Aunt Catherine, I just can't wait to get to heaven."

"Well, I can't either, Miss Kayla. Thank you for telling me what it's all about."

I believe my little Kayla has it right. What she was really saying is that heaven is better than the best you can imagine. Heaven is the ultimate grace gift from our God of all grace. Believe it, receive it, and live it. Heaven is more than enough to look forward to and much greater than the temporary things here on earth. Earth is not worth extending our roots into when compared to the glory of heaven. Kayla imagines chocolate drinking fountains and chocolate-chip-cookie rain. And maybe she's right. The Bible doesn't tell us about the fountains and the rain. But God does say heaven is our home, a place prepared for us by Jesus, where He will receive us to Himself.

Randy Alcorn, in his book *Heaven,* encourages us to use our imaginations when considering heaven: "We cannot anticipate or desire what we cannot imagine. That's why, I believe, God has given us glimpses of Heaven in the Bible—to fire up our imagination and kindle a desire for Heaven in our hearts."[1] Just think about the best you can imagine in heaven and know it will be more and better than that. Like Kayla said, "Everything is much, much better!"

✳

The man's pain was so excruciating, he could barely bring himself to a single thought. He knew he was dying because of what he'd done. Condemned to crucifixion, he was suffering the most horrible punishment imaginable.

He wasn't alone. Two others were also hanging on crosses. He had screamed insults at one of them—the one who hadn't done anything to deserve this punishment—just like everyone else in the crowd. "Who do you think you are? The Messiah? Sure! If you are the Messiah, why are you on a cross?" But even as the words came out, he knew he had it wrong. And in an instant, he realized the truth. *I've had it wrong my whole life. This one knows. He really is who He claimed to be. I can see it. I know it.*

Then, in the fog of his pain, he heard the other criminal shouting out abusive lies, hurling insults. He had to stop him. "Stop it—right now! Do you not even fear God, since you are under the same sentence of condemnation? We are suffering justly, for we are receiving what we deserve for our deeds; but this man has done nothing wrong."

Even as he said these words, he began to understand more of their significance. *I deserve to die. But this one is without sin. I believe he is a king with a kingdom.* He could think only of His name—Jesus. Then he knew what he must do. He cried out, "Jesus, remember me when You come in Your kingdom!"

And now, grace again ruled, even on wooden crosses of convicted criminals who were paying for their crimes. Jesus, in the midst of His own passion, carrying the sins of all humanity and paying their penalty, turned to one repentant criminal on a cross and said, "Truly I say to you, today you shall be with Me in Paradise."

Even His words, given through unspeakable pain, were filled with grace. Imagine what they must have meant to the criminal who was about to die on his own cross. Grace finds you wherever you are and goes out of its way to save you. And then grace carries you into heaven.

It's hard to imagine another world and another life when we are so present in this world. Life on earth is all we've known. But we've touched and tasted eternity as we've walked with God in the garden of grace, and someday, what we know here on earth will fade into the background, and heaven will be our home. Even time as we know it will be past, and we will live in the eternal realm.

Paul assures us that because we are justified by grace, we are made heirs according to the hope of eternal life (Titus 3:7). Eternal life is life that lasts forever. God's grace is the vehicle He uses to take us into eternity. The garden of grace is merely a glimpse of what is to come for us. We are looking forward to more than we realize.

Jesus, in the moments when He was close to His return home to heaven, called heaven *paradise.* When we think of paradise, a lush garden environment often comes to our minds. In the Jewish mind-set of Jesus' day, the imagery of paradise was developed from an ancient

Persian term reflecting on the Garden of Eden. And in fact, in the final chapter of Revelation, we are taken into the ultimate paradise with a sparkling clear river of life coming from God's throne, the tree of life, and the light of God Himself brightening all of heaven. In that view of heaven, we, the bondservants of God, are there with the Lord's name on our foreheads, signifying we are His. We are assured that we will see His face, and we will reign forever and ever. Paradise is the destiny of all those who have entered into the garden of God's grace.

✳

William Dorset, a Yorkshire farmer, was preaching one night and stated with conviction, "There is not a man or woman in all of London so far gone but that the grace of God can save them." His statement was considered quite radical, especially in light of a city with four million inhabitants and many caught in a sea of sin.

One young missionary woman could not stop thinking about his words. Finally, she went to Dorset and said, "I heard you preach last night, and I heard you say that there was not a man so far gone in all of London but that the grace of God could save him. Did you really mean it?"

Dorset replied, "Yes, I certainly meant it."

"Well," she said, "I am a missionary down in the East End of London, and I have found a man who says there is no hope for him. He is dying, and I cannot get him to believe there is any hope. I wish you would go see him."

Dorset agreed to go. The woman led the way down a narrow street to a filthy, abandoned building. "I think you'd better meet with him alone," she suggested. Dorset climbed five flights of stairs and found the poor man lying on a bed of straw. Through a life of wantonness and sin, he now had come to this sad estate, sick and dying and totally abandoned in an empty building. Mr. Dorset bent over him, leaned down, and whispered in his ear, "Friend."

Astonished, the young man said, "You are mistaken sir, in the person. You are in the wrong place."

"Why do you say that?" replied Dorset.

"Because sir, I have no friend. I am friendless."

"Young man, you do have a friend. His name is Christ. He is your friend, and He loves you."

"Christ doesn't love me. I've sinned against Him my entire life."

"It doesn't matter. He loves you anyway. He died for you. He loves you and wants to save you."

Dorset described the extravagant grace of a loving Savior in every way he knew. He read from the Bible. Soon, the truth dawned in the man's heart. He received Christ and was pierced with conviction over his sins. He said, "If only I could know that my father forgives me, I would die happy in this place."

Dorset replied, "I will go find your father and ask him to forgive you."

"Don't do that. My father has disinherited and disowned me. He has had my name taken off the family records and doesn't speak of me. I am as dead to him."

Determined, Mr. Dorset went to the West End of London and walked up a path to a beautiful house. A servant answered the door and led him to the drawing room. While Dorset waited, he noticed the apparent wealth of this home.

Finally, the master of the house entered the room and shook Dorset's hand. Dorset said, "Sir, you have a son named Joseph, do you not?"

Rage filled the man and he shouted, "No. He is dead to me. Worthless. Not to be relied on."

"Your son is sick and dying, sir."

"My Joseph is dying?"

"Yes. I am here because he is your boy, and he wants more than anything to know that you forgive him."

The father's countenance changed, and with tears rolling down his face, he cried out, "I would have forgiven him long ago had I known he desired my forgiveness. Forgive him? Yes, I forgive him. Can you take me to him?"

When the father reached his bedside, he hardly recognized his bruised and battered son.

"Father, forgive me."

"Oh, Joseph, I forgive you! I would have forgiven you long ago had I known you wanted it. Let me take you home."

"No father, I'm too ill. And I will die soon, but I will die happy, for I know you have forgiven me, and I know that God, through Christ, has forgiven me."

His father held him close, and soon he breathed his last, stepping from time into eternity.

✳

Just think about the details of this story, and you will understand the power of grace. Only the grace of God would move every person and circumstance to find a lost, dying young man in an obscure building and bring him together with his estranged father. God's grace will find you, save you, sustain you, and keep you. And ultimately grace carries you into heaven, as it did this young man, where you will live forever and ever with the one who loves you best.

When my mother and I sang "It Is Well with My Soul," our hearts were comforted by the words of hope. We learned later that the woman stepped into the presence of the Lord 30 minutes after we left the house. I was struck with God's timing and realized His awesome grace at work once again. Only God could bring us to that house at that time and arrange for us to sing a hymn to usher her into His presence. When someone dies, we arrange the funeral details. But God arranges heaven's welcome. I was humbled that Mother and I were granted the privilege of being His choir for those brief moments.

I am looking forward to heaven. More and more people I know live there now. And I am on my way there. And if you know the Lord, you're on your way there also. I can't wait to see the people who helped me grow in the Lord—men and women like Amy Carmichael, Charles Spurgeon, A.W. Tozer, Bill Bright, Fanny Crosby, Hannah Whitall Smith, Andrew Murray, R.A. Torrey, D.L. Moody, J. Edwin Orr, and Henri Nouwen. And then, what about those who have helped me grow in the Word of God, like David, Moses, Abraham, Abigail, Jeremiah, Paul, and Peter! But most of all, I look forward to eternal life with Jesus.

Do you ever wonder what Jesus thinks about and looks forward to? I often think of the day Jesus was talking with His disciples. He told them, "Where I am going, you cannot come." He knew He was on His way back home.

Peter said, "Lord, where are You going?"

Jesus answered, "Where I go, you cannot follow Me now; but you will follow later."

And now Jesus opens His heart for us to understand. Jesus wants us with Him, close, forever. He never lets us go, and even when we step from death to life, He is right there with us, ushering us into our eternal home. Jesus promised us an actual place He is preparing, where we will live with Him forever (John 14:2). He continues with an even greater promise, one that gives us a window into His deepest desire. He says, "I will come again and receive you to Myself, that where I am, there you may be also" (John 14:3).

Think about those words for a moment. Jesus is telling us that there will never be a time when we will be apart from Him. He is most looking forward to our being with Him forever. These words prove it. We are with Him now. Even in death, His hand is extended, and He will take us into heaven. He is saying, "I always want you with Me. Wherever I am, you are there too." Oh, what comfort I find in His promise to receive me to Himself.

✳

A woman diagnosed with a terminal disease presented her pastor with an unusual request: "I want to be buried with a fork in my right hand." She told her pastor about her favorite part of any meal—the moment when someone says, "Keep your fork." Those words assured her of a wonderful dessert just ahead. She said, "I want people to wonder about that fork in my hand. Tell them, 'The best is yet to come.'"

Nothing compares with heaven, our eternal home. In the garden of grace, we catch glimpses of the beauty and bounty that lie ahead for us. Joni Eareckson Tada speaks of our anticipation of heaven: "The best we can hope for in this life is a knothole peek at the shining realities ahead. Yet a glimpse is enough. It's enough to convince our hearts that whatever sufferings and sorrows currently assail us aren't worthy of comparison to that which waits over the horizon."

And so, dear friend, get ready for the best God, in His matchless grace, has to offer when you step into heaven. For you will finally be home. Always remember this world is not your home. In fact, Octavius Winslow calls our life on earth a place of exile and a strange land:

> Earth shall not always be our place of exile; we shall not always sing the Lord's song in a strange land, nor always shed these tears...Each trembling step of faith, each holy aspiration of love, each sin subdued, each foe vanquished, each trial past, each temptation baffled, is bringing us nearer and still nearer to the bright threshold of glory.[2]

I love how my one friend responds when I ask him, "How are you?" He says, "Just one step closer to heaven."

Dear friend, I want to encourage you to hold to the hope of heaven when you are walking in the garden of grace. Are you discouraged today? Had you thought perhaps there was nothing that could bring brightness to the clouds in your life? You have a hope that is literally out of this world! Look up and take heart in the fact of heaven. Heaven is one of God's greatest gifts of grace. Believe it, receive it, and live it. One day you will step from time into eternity. As Randy Alcorn says, "Moving day is coming. The dark winter is about to be magically transformed into spring. One day soon you will be home—for the first time."[3] In the garden of grace, we always have our eyes fixed on eternity, knowing at any time God can call us home. Then you can breathe the deepest sigh of relief and say with true joy, "I'm home."

Many years ago, while on staff with the Josh McDowell Ministry, I was in a head-on collision. My head was all bandaged up, and I looked a sight. Josh came to me and said, "Catherine, I think you need to go home for a while."

I said, "I want to go home. I need my mother." I thought of only one thing on the plane ride home—getting off that plane and seeing my mother. When she saw me, she held me close, tight in her arms. I thought she would never let me go. When we got home, she marched me into my bedroom, pulled back the covers, and helped me into bed. I leaned back resting my head on the soft pillows and thought, *I'm home.*

I believe that is the way we will feel when we get to heaven. A sense of rest, joy, and even exuberance will be ours as we breathe that sigh of relief and say, "I'm finally home."

Some Alpine shepherds have a beautiful custom of ending their day by singing an evening farewell to one another. Dusk comes, and they gather their flocks together. And leading them down the mountain paths, they sing this song:

"Hitherto hath the Lord helped us. Let us praise His name!"

And at last with a sweet courtesy, as they head toward their respective homes, they sing to one another the friendly farewell:

"Goodnight! Goodnight!"

The words are replaced and repeated by echoes, and from side to side, through the hills and valleys, the song reverberates sweetly and softly until the music dies away in the distance.

And so for us, as we live day by day in this garden of grace until one day He comes for us, let us also call out to one another. Through the light of the day, the present darkness will become vocal with our many voices, encouraging all pilgrims to grow in grace and faithfully walk with their Lord in His grace land.

We will experience a new grace when all our voices join together in a hurricane of hallelujahs breaking "in thundering waves around the sapphire throne, and then as the morning breaks we shall find ourselves at the margin of the sea of glass, crying, with the redeemed host,

> Blessing, and honor, and glory,
> be unto Him that sitteth on the throne,
> and to the Lamb forever and ever!
> This my song through endless ages,
> Jesus led me all the way.[4]

"And again they shouted, hallelujah!" (Revelation 19:3 NIV).

APPENDIX

Our Quiet Time Together

The following is an example of how I led a group of 500 women through a quiet time at a women's retreat in Murrieta, California.

✳

Let's begin with *Prepare Your Heart*. "Lord, speak to me today as I draw near to You. Thank You for being here. I love spending time with You." Then think about these words from one of my favorite devotionals, *My Utmost for His Highest*, by Oswald Chambers: "*Cast thy burden upon the Lord*...If we undertake the work of God and get out of touch with Him, the sense of responsibility will be overwhelmingly crushing; but if we roll back on God that which He has put upon us, He takes away the sense of responsibility by bringing us into a realization of Himself." After reading Chambers' meaningful words, you might write your thoughts in your journal. I like to pull out my *Quiet Time Notebook,* turn to the journal pages in the *Prepare Your Heart* section, and write a prayer. You might write something like this: *Lord, thank You for reminding me that I need to give You my burdens. I was actually feeling overwhelmed today by some responsibilities. But I realize You want to carry every burden so that I may easily run my race with You.*

Then, move to *Read and Study God's Word.* Choose a psalm, such as Psalm 34, as your Bible reading plan for the day and begin reading. Verses 17-18 are significant for us today: "The righteous cry, and the Lord hears and delivers them out of all their troubles. The Lord is near to the brokenhearted and saves those who are crushed in spirit." Write out your favorite verses in your journal or *Quiet Time Notebook* and then their meaning to you, something like this: "These verses comfort me today. What a joy to know that even if I can't physically see the Lord, I am assured of His nearness, especially when I am broken and crushed. He is inviting me to cry out to Him and promising me that when He hears, He delivers. *Lord, I am counting on these promises today.*"

Then, *Adore God in Prayer.* I like to pray for my family and friends, pray for other urgent needs, and write out some of my prayer requests in my *Quiet Time Notebook.*

In *Yield Yourself to God,* apply what you have learned in the psalm for the day and talk with God about some of the areas where perhaps you feel brokenhearted, giving each burden to the Lord. Then surrender, giving way to His ways in your life.

In *Enjoy His Presence,* say, *Thank You, Lord, for showing me Your nearness today. Help me remember You throughout the day.*

Finally, in *Rest in His Love,* carry in your heart the promise that He will hear and deliver you, and rest in knowing He is with you.

This is only one example of how I spend quiet time with the Lord. Quiet times may last from ten minutes to two hours, depending on your schedule and season in life. You can use other devotionals or Bible reading plans as you spend time with God.

MORE AFFIRMATIONS OF GRACE

Because of God's grace...

I live forever in God's unmerited favor and always enjoy His smile.

I am in the environment that God has perfectly designed to help me grow spiritually mature.

I am the recipient of God's lavish and extravagant gifts of grace.

I am blessed with every spiritual blessing in the heavenly places in Christ.

I have a spiritual inheritance, reserved in heaven, and I have riches that last forever.

I have received everything I need to live the victorious and abundant Christian life.

I am a recipient of God's unconditional love.

I am given Jesus.

I can now enjoy an intimate, ongoing, vibrant relationship with Christ.

I am forgiven all my sins, redeemed, justified, sanctified, and righteous in God's sight.

I am blessed with eternal life with the Lord in heaven.

I am secure and safe in God's everlasting arms.

I am a saint and a citizen of the kingdom of God.

I am a member of the family of God.

I am a brand-new person—not an alteration of the old, but completely new.

I am given new life in Christ.

I am set free from the power of sin, so I can say yes to God and no to sin.

I am set free to love and serve the Lord.

I am given the indwelling Holy Spirit and have become a temple of God's Spirit.

I can be controlled and empowered by God through the Holy Spirit.

I am given strength through Christ to overcome every obstacle and challenge.

I have a new identity in Christ—I'm accepted in Him forever.

I am united with Christ, and it is no longer I who live, but Christ lives in me.

I am beautiful, and I shine with the holiness and glory of Christ.

I am a member of the bride of Jesus Christ, now royalty, and His princess.

I am a part of the church of Jesus Christ.

I have a future and a hope.

I am given the gift of God's Word,
including His magnificent promises.

I am given understanding of God's Word.

I am given free access to the throne of grace,
finding help in my times of need.

I am given a life with meaning, significance,
and complete satisfaction and fulfillment.

I am a trophy of God's grace.

I am God's work in progress, being
transformed more and more to be like
Christ.

I can thrive, grow, and bear fruit even in
adverse circumstances.

I am given the outrageous, exciting joy of
the Lord, which is my strength.

I am given the renewing and reviving gift of
a new day regardless of what I face in life.

I am now able to rest in Christ, content and
peaceful, enjoying Him forever.

I am given the calm assurance of Christ,
who overcomes in every situation.

I am given spiritual armor for protection in
spiritual warfare.

I am given the opportunity daily to share
God's grace with others.

I am given a high calling, and I share in
God's plans, dreams, and desires.

I am given the hope of heaven, my eternal
home with Christ.

God's grace…Believe it, receive it, and live it.

NOTES

Chapter 1: In the Garden of Grace

1. A.W. Tozer, *The Knowledge of the Holy* (New York: Harper & Row, 1961), 103.
2. Chuck Swindoll, *The Grace Awakening* (Nashville: Thomas Nelson, 2003), 15.
3. Joseph R. Cooke, *Celebration of Grace* (Milton-Freewater, OR: Outwest Printing, 1991), 13.
4. Cathleen Falsani, *Sin Boldly* (Grand Rapids: Zondervan, 2008), 11.
5. Brian H. Edwards, *Grace—Amazing Grace* (Leominster, MA: Day One, 2003), 4.
6. David Jeremiah, *Captured by Grace* (Brentwood: Integrity, 2006), 13.
7. Philip Yancey, *What's So Amazing About Grace?* (Grand Rapids: Zondervan, 1997), 15.
8. Cooke, *Celebration of Grace,* 201.

Chapter 2: Grow Deep in the Garden of Grace

1. Dallas Willard, *Renovation of the Heart* (Colorado Springs: NavPress, 2002), 22, 159.
2. draltang.blogspot.com/2008/02/spiritual-formation-education-of-heart.html.
3. Greg L. Hawkins and Cally Parkinson, *Reveal* (Barrington, IL: Willow Creek Association, 2007), 33-47.
4. Greg L. Hawkins and Cally Parkinson, *Follow Me* (Barrington, IL: Willow Creek Association, 2008), 27-28.

Chapter 3: Living Extravagantly in the Garden

1. Brother Yun, *Living Water* (Grand Rapids: Zondervan, 2008), 93.
2. Hawkins and Parkinson, *Follow Me,* 105.
3. For more information about having a quiet time, see *Six Secrets to a Powerful Quiet Time* (Eugene, OR: Harvest House, 2006).
4. You can join quiet time studies online at www.cathscommunity.com.

5. Some of my favorites are Precept Upon Precept studies, Howard Hendricks's workshops, John Maxwell DVD series, and conferences on DVD like Preach the Word from Harvest Christian Fellowship. Quiet Time Ministries also offers many DVD quiet time studies at www.myquiettime.com.

6. To grow in your beliefs, see my books *Knowing and Loving the Bible, Set My Heart on Fire, Trusting in the Names of God,* and *Passionate Prayer,* all published by Harvest House.

7. Falsani, *Sin Boldly,* 9.

8. Hawkins and Parkinson, *Follow Me,* 47.

9. Oswald Chambers, *My Utmost for His Highest* (Uhrichsville, OH: Barbour, 1963), 151.

10. Quoted in Miles J. Stanford, *The Green Letters—Principles of Spiritual Growth* (Grand Rapids: Zondervan, 1975), 10-11.

Chapter 4: Caterpillars Can Fly

1. Cited in Elisabeth Elliot, *A Chance to Die* (Old Tappan, NJ: Revell, 1987), 22.

2. Amy Carmichael, *Mimosa* (Fort Washington, PA: Christian Literature Crusade), 11.

3. Carmichael, *Mimosa,* 18.

4. Willard, *Renovation of the Heart,* 66.

5. Cooke, *Celebration of Grace,* 125.

6. Willard, *Renovation of the Heart,* 138.

7. Deion Sanders with Him Nelson Black, *Power, Money, and Sex* (Nashville: Word, 1999).

Chapter 5: It's Not Your Life

1. Steve McVey, *Grace Walk* (Eugene, OR: Harvest House, 1995), 13.

2. McVey, *Grace Walk,* 27-28.

3. Steve McVey, *Grace Walk* (Eugene, OR: Harvest House, 1995), back cover.

4. Major W. Ian Thomas, *The Saving Life of Christ* (Grand Rapids: Zondervan, 1961), 10.

5. Elliot, *A Chance to Die,* 15.

6. Brother Yun, *The Heavenly Man* (Raleigh, NC: Monarch Books, 2002), 13.

7. Attributed variously to A.A. Whiddington, A.B. Simpson, and Frances E. Bolton.

Chapter 6: Beauty for Ashes

1. Sheri Rose Shepherd, *My Prince Will Come* (Colorado Springs: Multnomah Books, 2005), 13.

2. Lewis Sperry Chafer, *Systematic Theology,* vol. 2 (Wheaton: Victor Books, 1988), 333.

3. Max Lucado, *In the Grip of Grace* (Dallas: Word, 1996), xi.

4. Nancy Stafford, *Beauty by the Book* (Sisters, OR: Multnomah, 2002), 36.

5. Stafford, *Beauty by the Book,* 110.

6. Shepherd, *My Prince Will Come,* 39.

Chapter 7: Riches for Poverty

1. Helen Kooiman Hosier, *100 Christian Women Who Changed the 20th Century* (Grand Rapids: Revell, 2000), 210.
2. Hosier, *100 Christian Women Who Changed the 20th Century,* 211.
3. Hosier, *100 Christian Women Who Changed the 20th Century,* 211.
4. John MacArthur, *Twelve Extraordinary Women* (Nashville: Thomas Nelson, 2005), 191.

Chapter 8: Seasons of the Soul

1. Quoted in Hosier, *100 Christian Women Who Changed the 20th Century,* 37.
2. Chuck Swindoll, *Growing Strong in the Seasons of Life* (Portland: Multnomah Press, 1983), 13.

Chapter 9: The Door Is Always Open

1. Jerry Bridges, *Transforming Grace* (Colorado Springs: NavPress, 2008), 214.
2. Quoted in Ken Gire, *Between Heaven and Earth* (San Francisco: HarperSanFrancisco, 1997), 189.
3. Edwards, *Grace—Amazing Grace,* 280-81.
4. Edwards, *Grace—Amazing Grace,* 295.

Chapter 10: Theology of the New Day

1. Quoted in Elizabeth R. Skoglund, *Found Faithful* (Grand Rapids: Discovery House, 2003), 190.
2. Quoted in Skoglund, *Found Faithful,* 195-96.
3. Gigi Graham Tchividjian, *Weather of the Heart* (Portland: Multnomah Press, 1991), 42-43.
4. Gordon MacDonald, *A Resilient Life* (Nashville: Thomas Nelson, 2004), vii.
5. Kay Arthur, *Lord, I Need Grace to Make It* (Portland: Multnomah Press, 1989), 13.

Chapter 11: Crazy for Jesus

1. Anne Graham Lotz, *Why?* (Nashville: Thomas Nelson, 2004), 24.
2. Anne Graham Lotz, *Just Give Me Jesus* (Nashville: Thomas Nelson, 2009), vi.
3. www.christianbookpreviews.com
4. Stefanie Kelly, *I Know He Knows,* ©1997 Silky Tunes. Used by permission. www.stefaniekelly.com.
5. Sherwood E. Wirt, *Jesus, Man of Joy* (Eugene, OR: Harvest House, 1999), 59.
6. Beth Moore, *Jesus, the One and Only* (Nashville: Broadman & Holman, 2002), ix.
7. Francis Chan, *Crazy Love* (Colorado Springs: David C. Cook, 2008), 61.
8. Author unknown.
9. A.W. Tozer, *The Root of the Righteous* (Camp Hill: PA: Christian Publications, 1986), 181.

10. Anne Graham Lotz, *I Saw the Lord* (Grand Rapids: Zondervan, 2006), 69.

11. David Bryant, *Christ Is All!* (New Providence, NJ: New Providence, 2005), 398.

12. Chan, *Crazy Love,* 70-72,75.

Chapter 12: The Fine Art of Gracing Another

1. Patsy Clairmont, et al., *Extravagant Grace* (Grand Rapids: Zondervan, 2000), 68.

2. I share the story of learning about faith from Ney Bailey in *A Woman's Heart That Dances* (Eugene, OR: Harvest House, 2009).

3. Clairmont, et al., *Extravagant Grace,* 68-70.

4. Falsani, *Sin Boldly,* 91.

5. Hosier, *100 Christian Women Who Changed the 20th Century,* 205.

Chapter 13: Dreaming God's Dreams

1. Steven J. Patrick, blog.seattlepi.com/theconstantvalentine/archives/166554.asp?from =blog_last3.

2. Noel Piper, *Faithful Women & Their Extraordinary God* (Wheaton: Crossway Books, 2005), 44.

3. Hosier, *100 Christian Women Who Changed the 20th Century,* 289.

4. Blanche A.F. Pigott, *I. Lilias Trotter* (London: Marshall, Morgan & Scott, 1929), 9-10.

5. Pigott, *I. Lilias Trotter,* 11.

6. Miriam Huffman Rockness, comp. and ed., *A Blossom in the Desert* (Grand Rapids: Discovery House, 2007), 21.

7. Miriam Huffman Rockness, *A Passion for the Impossible* (Wheaton: Harold Shaw, 1999), 288-89.

8. Hosier, *100 Christian Women Who Changed the 20th Century,* 290.

9. Rockness, *A Blossom in the Desert,* 24.

10. Piper, *Faithful Women & Their Extraordinary God,* 63.

Chapter 14: Chocolate Drinking Fountains

1. Randy Alcorn, *Heaven* (Carol Stream, IL: Tyndale House, 2004), 16.

2. Octavius Winslow, *Help Heavenward* (Carlisle, PA: Banner of Truth Trust, 2000), 10.

3. Randy Alcorn, *Heaven,* 22.

4. Mrs. Charles E. Cowman, *Streams in the Desert* (Los Angeles: The Oriental Missionary Society, 1925), 376.

About the Author

Catherine Martin is a summa cum laude graduate of Bethel Theological Seminary with a master of arts degree in theological studies. She is founder and president of Quiet Time Ministries, director of women's ministries at Southwest Community Church in Indian Wells, California, and adjunct faculty member of Biola University. She is the author of many books and is senior editor for *Enriching Your Quiet Time* quarterly magazine. As a popular speaker at retreats and conferences, Catherine challenges others to seek God and love Him with all of their heart, soul, mind, and strength. For more information about Catherine, visit www.quiettime.org, www.catherinemartinonline.com, and www.cathsblog.com.

About Quiet Time Ministries

Quiet Time Ministries is a nonprofit organization offering resources for your quiet time. Visit us online at www.quiettime.org. The Quiet Time Ministries Resource and Training Center, located in Bermuda Dunes, California, offers conferences and workshops to encourage others in their relationship with the Lord.

Quiet Time Ministries
Post Office Box 14007
Palm Desert, CA 92255
1-800-925-6458
760-772-2357
www.quiettime.org

More Great Books by Catherine Martin
from Harvest House Publishers

Passionate Prayer
This intensely practical book encourages you to develop greater passion for God and for communion with Him. You will discover the power of talking with God, be reminded of His promises when you pray, and experience the privilege of an intimate prayer relationship.
> Companion volume: Passionate Prayer—A Quiet Time Experience

Trusting in the Names of God
Catherine presents the many names of God, describes how they reveal His character, and teaches that by trusting in them you can better understand who God is.
> Companion volume: Trusting in the Names of God—A Quiet Time Experience

A Woman's Heart That Dances
Do you long to feel chosen, to dance with the One who can lead you through the intricate turns of your life? Join Catherine as she explores the image of the dance, and discover how you can recognize and respond to the Lord's surprising invitations to you. You'll engage in the romance and adventure of an intimate, personal relationship with Him, and you'll learn to follow His lead as He choreographs the story of your life.

Set My Heart on Fire
Thoroughly scriptural and theologically conservative, this passionate invitation to a life of obedience and holiness uses biblical teaching, inspirational stories, and personal anecdotes to gently but effectively lead you into a deeper walk with the Lord.

Knowing and Loving the Bible
This powerful, interactive journey transforms reading and studying the Bible into acts of love and brings you closer to God as you discover nourishment for daily living and build a foundation on His promises.

Six Secrets to a Powerful Quiet Time
If you desire a close walk with God, a rich devotion time, and the joy of pursuing God, you will find inspiration, tools, and encouragement while exploring the *Six Secrets to a Powerful Quiet Time.*